KU-211-217

JOSEPH CRAWHALL

1 8 6 1 – 1 9 1 3

1
Mendelssohn
Joseph Crawhall
(1861–1913)
c.1882
Photograph
Central Library, Newcastle
upon Tyne

JOSEPH CRAWHALL

1861 – 1913

ONE OF THE GLASGOW BOYS

by

VIVIEN HAMILTON

JOHN MURRAY
in association with
GLASGOW MUSEUMS AND
ART GALLERIES

© Glasgow Museums and Art Galleries 1990

First published in 1990
by John Murray (Publishers) Ltd,
50 Albemarle Street, London W1X 4BD
in association with Glasgow Museums and Art Galleries

JOSEPH CRAWHALL *an exhibition*
sponsored by BMW (GB) Limited

John Murray ISBN 0 7195 4827 6
Glasgow Museums and Art Galleries ISBN 0 902752 40 5

All rights reserved
Unauthorised duplication contravenes
applicable laws

British Library Cataloguing in Publication Data

Hamilton, Vivien
Joseph Crawhall 1861–1913: one of Glasgow's Boys.
1. Scottish paintings. Crawhall, Joseph, *1861–1913*
I. Title
759.2911

ISBN 0-7195-4827-6

Photoset by Rowland Phototypesetting Ltd,
Bury St Edmunds, Suffolk
Printed in Great Britain by
Butler and Tanner Ltd, Frome and London

CONTENTS

For Mum, Anne and Raymond
and in memory of Dad

PREFACE

and

ACKNOWLEDGEMENTS

The Glasgow shipowner Sir William Burrell's collection of the works of Joseph Crawhall is the largest and finest in existence – a collection devotedly brought together over more than seventy years and one which today contains many Crawhalls formerly in the collections of other Glasgow patrons. It was entirely appropriate that, late in 1986, the idea was first put forward that a major loan exhibition of the works of the artist be held at the Burrell Collection during Glasgow's reign as European City of Culture in 1990.

On my appointment at the Burrell Collection in 1987 I began to pursue research on Crawhall, an artist who, I discovered, was with good reason known as 'The Great Silence'. Apart from a few early articles, brief accounts by contemporaries and the groundwork provided by Adrian Bury's monograph of 1958, it soon became apparent that little was known and, unfortunately, little in the way of documentary material remained extant. It would have been a much simpler task to have produced, as is customary, an exhibition catalogue concentrating on the works rather than the artist himself. It appeared, however, that such a publication would not be appropriate. Countless written, telephone and personal enquiries about Joseph Crawhall are received at the Burrell Collection each week. It is hoped, therefore, that this monograph will go some way to satisfying the many people fascinated by the artist's work but for whom nothing has been available in print for many years.

An archive has been founded at the Burrell Collection bringing together photographs, newscuttings and reviews, and copies of the archival documents that survive. It houses too copies of articles and books – the primary and secondary sources that mention Crawhall or throw some light on his character. This archive is continuing to grow and the author would be delighted to hear from anyone who could contribute to it in any way.

My grateful thanks go to the many individuals and institutions who have contributed to the organisation of the exhibition and to the preparation of this publication. To the private collectors – most of whom wish to remain anonymous – for their kindness, patience and hospitality, for allowing me to see and photograph their collections and for agreeing to lend to the exhibition and be parted from their favourite works for a period of four months; Sir Norman and Lady Macfarlane; Bill Smith of Robert Fleming Holdings; Mr Paul Mellon and Beverly Carter; and the many members of the Crawhall family, some of whom I have met, others with whom I have corresponded, who have racked their brains and searched their attics.

For assistance with research, the provision of photographs and in many cases for lending to the exhibition I wish to thank: Antony Griffiths, Print Room, British Museum; Halina Graham and Andrea George, Cecil Higgins Art Gallery; Sarah Richardson, Laing Art Gallery; Tessa Sidey, Birmingham Museum and Art Gallery; Andrea Kerr, Kirkcaldy Museum and Art Gallery; Clara Young and David Scruton, Dundee Museum and Art Gallery; Hugh Macandrew, Margaret Ross and Julie Murphy, National Gallery of Scotland; Dr Thomson, Dr Marshall and Helen Smailes of the Scottish National Portrait Gallery; Chris Allen, Martin Hopkinson, Pamela Robertson and June Barrie, Hunterian Art Gallery; Pat Clegg, Harrogate Art Gallery; Alexander Robertson and Corinne Miller, Leeds City Art Gallery; R. J. Malden, Paisley Museum and Art Gallery; Gregory Smith and Jennifer Harris, Whitworth Art Gallery; R. M. Doughty of Berwick upon Tweed Borough Museum and Art Gallery; Anne MacPhee and Xanthe Brooke, Walker Art Gallery; and the staff of the Tate Gallery, London.

I also wish to thank the staff of the following libraries: British Library; National Art Library, Victoria and Albert Museum; Joan Harvey, Witt Collection, Courtauld Institute; Frank Manders and the Local Studies staff at Newcastle Central Library; Glasgow University Library, especially Elizabeth Watson, David Weston, Philip Escreet and Nigel Thorpe of Special Collections; Jennifer Booth, the Tate Archive; Mrs Alexander of Frame and Co. Chartered Surveyors (archives of Royal Scottish Society of Painters in Watercolours); Denis Peel, Society of Antiquaries, Newcastle upon Tyne; Margaret Burden, Central Library, Morpeth; and Dale Russell, Jean Cullen and Margaret Cavers, Broughton House.

Throughout the period of research I have benefited from the help and knowledge of many people: Maria Beston; Brian Allen; Elizabeth Hancock; Roger Billcliffe; Michael and Sue Crawhall; Jane Hickman; Greg Shapland; A. H. Tweddle; Geoffrey Greed; Kenneth McConkey; Linda E. Wilkinson; The Lord of Clandermond; Ailsa Tanner; Joanne Cox; and Kenneth Varty. Fiona Macsporran has shared with me her extensive knowledge of Walton and the Glasgow Boys and suggested many avenues of research; and Mrs A. Morrison has very patiently and with great success waded through many 'years' of newspapers to discover the exhibition reviews that shed much light on how Crawhall's work was received by his contemporaries.

I also wish to thank the many dealers and auctioneers who have helped me trace the whereabouts of works by Crawhall and thereby build up a much fuller picture of the artist's oeuvre: Barclay Lennie, Ewan and Carol Mundy; Cyril Gerber; Andrew Whitfield; Guy Peploe; the staff of Spink, London; Mrs Susannah

Jackson; and Graham Reid and Susannah Pollen. In 1985 the Fine Art Society organised a small but important exhibition of the work of Joseph Crawhall and I am very much indebted to John Shand-Kydd and Andrew Mackintosh Patrick for sharing their knowledge with me and for suggesting the Fine Art Society as a suitable second venue for the exhibition.

One of the most rewarding aspects of working in a museum is the teamwork – there are usually many brains and many hands involved in each and every project. I wish to thank my colleagues on the staff of Glasgow Museums and Art Galleries for being such a wonderful team. My thanks go to all members of staff but especial thanks for assistance with both the exhibition and the publication to: Anne Donald; Hugh Stevenson; Jean Walsh; James MacGowan and the team of gilders; Rhona White for two years of work conserving the Crawhalls in preparation for the exhibition; to the photographers for working often in adverse conditions – James Stewart and Maureen, Ina, Ellen and John; Geraldine Glynn; Judith Wilder; and to the patient readers of my text – Rosemary Watt, Nicholas Pearce, James Thomson; and to Patricia Bascom for the Index. Martin Hopkinson also read the text and made many suggestions as did my patient editor, John Murray. I thank all the above for their help, advice and suggestions but must state that the faults that remain are those of the author.

This book is dedicated to the people without whom it could never have been written – my thanks, mere words, are not enough for their love, encouragement and understanding, and for their support.

VIVIEN HAMILTON
January 1990

Sponsored by BMW (GB) Limited

5 July–26 August 1990: The Burrell Collection, Glasgow
4–29 September 1990: The Fine Art Society, London

We at BMW (GB) Limited are delighted to sponsor the Joseph Crawhall Exhibition at the Burrell Collection in Glasgow and at the Fine Art Society in London.

It is very exciting for our company to support this extensive and diverse exhibition in two such important and beautiful galleries and we are proud to be associated with Glasgow Museums & Art Galleries and the Fine Art Society.

We hope that visitors to this exhibition will greatly enjoy the range of pictures on view, illustrating Crawhall's travels, love of horses and other animals, his humour and brilliant draughtsmanship.

BMW, a truly European company, with its headquarters in Germany and dealerships throughout the world, is especially proud to participate in Glasgow's reign as the European City of Culture during 1990.

Paul Layzell
Managing Director
BMW (GB) Limited

January 1990

FOREWORD

by

ROGER BILLCLIFFE

Of the twenty or so artists whose friendship and shared ideals created the Glasgow school of painters, the two watercolourists, Joseph Crawhall and Arthur Melville, have always demanded individual attention. It is not just the medium in which they excelled which has marked them as different from their friends. It is, I think, more directly related to the commitment they brought to their work and the consistent quality of vision and technique which they exercised throughout their relatively short working lives.

Crawhall was not the most gregarious of men, but in his early years he became close enough to James Guthrie and E. A. Walton to become their regular companion on their summer painting trips. In later life, in Tangier, he could be a stimulating and energetic companion of John Lavery, especially when horses were at the centre of the day and he could show off his skills as a jockey and extend his talents to help less gifted riders master their mounts. At other times he would retreat into monosyllabic communication and, when painting, shut himself away from other people, preferring the company of animals.

Out of this silent and solitary withdrawal came a series of intense, minutely described paintings, which seem all the more remarkable when one considers their medium. Crawhall's use of watercolour was by no means traditional. Like Melville, Crawhall invented his own vocabulary, using colour and wash like no other watercolour painter before him. In contrast to the 'blottesque' handling of Melville, the tight drawing and fine detail of Crawhall's studies of birds and animals impose another kind of discipline on the artist. Where other painters can take advantage of the sometimes unpredictable nature of watercolour, Crawhall handled the medium with almost unprecedented control, straining the versatility of the medium to its limits. He coaxed out of it a new delicacy, often using a fine linen instead of paper. Ravishing as these works on linen are, they make us more aware of his power in resolving the further difficulties which such an unyielding surface must have presented.

The naturalist paintings for which the Glasgow Boys are now famous were produced in a short, if intense, period of their lives in the mid-1880s. Working alongside Guthrie and his friends at Crowland and Cockburnspath, Crawhall was taken away from the tradition of book-illustration in which he grew up and introduced to the new world of easel painting, annual exhibitions and painting excursions in the summer where the aim was to make enough notes to sustain an artist for a winter's work in his studio. Crawhall responded well enough, experimenting with painting in oil and even producing the occasional large canvas for the Glasgow Institute or the Academy. All the Boys were to try their hands at watercolour, probably encouraged by Melville, but Crawhall and Walton produced some of their most successful naturalist paintings in this medium. Crawhall was never very relaxed working in oil and he found watercolour was the most natural way for him to capture the realism of the light and the life of the country which was at the core of the Glasgow Boys' achievement. Gradually, most of the Boys drifted away from their ideals of 'rustic naturalism' towards other kinds of painting, which demanded less of the painter and also helped them more easily to sustain a living. Crawhall, too, moved away from the naturalism of Bastien-Lepage, but in many ways his work became more difficult to understand, rather than more accessible.

It is easy to look at his watercolours of horses and birds and accept them as articulate and elegant examples of picture-making. To me there is another and more profound aspect of these paintings. If Crawhall merely wanted a career as a successful and acclaimed painter of animal studies, he could have achieved it quite easily without embarking on the weeks and months of concentration and nervous exhaustion which went into his work. The solitary side of his character possibly encouraged his adoption of an obsessively detailed technique. He established a rapport between himself and his subjects which, I think, drove him to attempt to re-create them on paper. *A Mallard Rising*, *The Spangled Cock*, *The Governess Cart* are the quintessential studies of these animals. Drawn mainly from memory over a period of several weeks, they are a distillation of the artist's prodigious knowledge about each bird or horse – if not *all* such animals. They go far beyond the record of some particular incident, as in the Cockburnspath paintings, making a highly personal statement about the beauty, mystery and power of the world about us. Crawhall, like many artists, would never have been able to talk or write about his respect for, and love and awe of, the natural world. His paintings are his way of conveying his feelings when confronted by the sheen of a horse's coat or drops of water lying on a bird's feathers. His paintings are his attempt to make something as beautiful as his subject matter by forcing himself to overcome the almost insuperable difficulties which were implicit in his chosen medium.

Crawhall was not as unremittingly intense and isolated as his contemporaries sometimes remembered him. His sketchbooks show a man with a gift for capturing the funny side of life in a few deft strokes. Often he would tear out these sketches and send them to brothers and sisters, nephews and nieces, along with letters covered with amusing doodles and caricatures. He spoke with his pen and his brush. 'Creeps' and 'The Great Silence' he might have been when in company –

alone in his studio with a brush or pen to hand, or out riding in Yorkshire or Morocco, he could communicate with greater power than many of his more loquacious friends. Our regret now is that he painted so little and our consolation is that each of these beautiful watercolours is unsurpassable. In detail and power of vision, Crawhall has no masters and few equals.

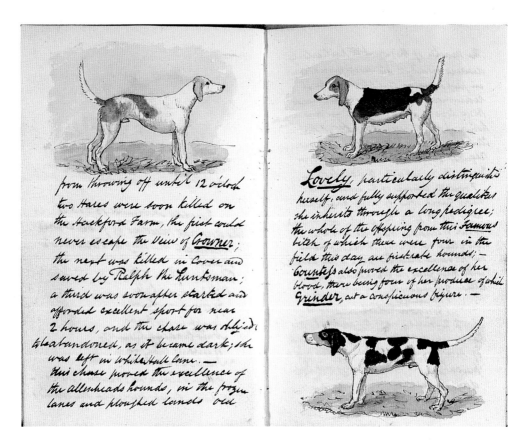

2
Joseph Crawhall
(1793–1853)
'Crowner, Lovely and
Grinder'
1831
Ink and wash on paper,
15.6×20.0
Private Collection

from throwing off until 12 o'clock
two Hares were soon killed on
the Hackford Farm, the first could
never escape the view of Crowner;
the next was killed in Cover and
saved by Ralph the Huntsman;
a third was soon after started and
afforded excellent sport for near
2 hours, and the chase was obliged
to be abandoned, as it became dark; she
was left in Whitehall Lane. —
This chase proved the excellence of
the Allenheads hounds, in the frozen
lanes and ploughed lands old

Lovely, particularly distinguished
herself, and fully supported the qualities
she inherits through a long pedigree;
the whole of the offspring from this famous
bitch of which there were four in the
field this day are first-rate hounds; —
Countess also proved the excellence of her
blood, there being four of her produce of whom
Grinder, cut a conspicuous figure. —

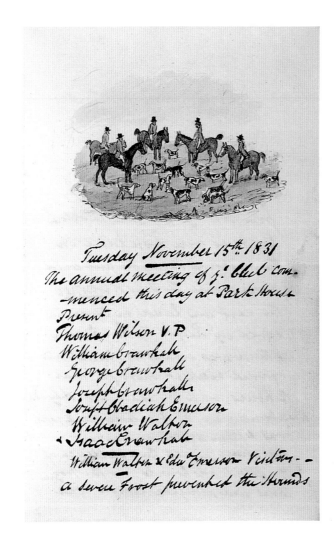

3
Joseph Crawhall
(1793–1853)
The Meet
1831
Ink and wash on paper,
15.6×20.0
Private Collection

Tuesday November 15th 1831
The annual meeting of ye club com-
-menced this day at Park House
Present
Thomas Wilson V.P
William Crawhall
George Crawhall
Joseph Crawhall
Joseph Obadiah Emerson
William Walton
Isaac Crawhall
William Walton & Edw Emerson Visitors —
a severe Frost prevented the Hounds

CHAPTER

1

THREE GENERATIONS

Unknown all his life to the general public, and even now only
appreciated by his fellow artists, he certainly was a man of genius,
if any painter ever merited the term.[1]

R. B. Cunninghame Graham, *Writ in Sand*

Joseph Crawhall was an enigma to his contemporaries and still remains one
today. He was a man of medium height, with heavy eyebrows, deep-set eyes,
high cheek-bones and a prominent chin (pl 1). The penetrating gaze saw all,
but Crawhall the man communicated little. By reputation a wit, he was by
nature reticent. The artist John Lavery called him 'The Great Silence' and his
friend Cunninghame Graham remarked that 'no one ever better merited the
name.'[2] It has been said that 'drawing became like thinking to him, and . . . just as
subconsciously. It was his speech. His pencil was to him what the tongue is to
other men.'[3]

Joseph Crawhall was born on 20 August 1861 at Wansbeck House, 120
Newgate Street, Morpeth, the second son and fourth child of Joseph Crawhall
(1821–96) and Margaret Boyd (1833–1928). Like so many of the Glasgow Boys,
with whom he was associated, Joseph Crawhall was the son of a prosperous
middle-class family whose wealth depended on the continued industrial and
commercial success of the Victorian Empire. Some idea of the standard of living
and the scale of the household can be ascertained from the 1861 Census – a census
taken just before Joseph's birth. His father Joseph Crawhall (thirty-nine), Master
Roper, and his wife Margaret (twenty-seven) lived with their two children:
Elspeth (five), a 'scholar', and Judith (eleven months). There were three unmarried

female servants: a housemaid, Margaret (twenty-two) of Newcastle, and her sister Mary (fifteen) the waiting maid; and Eliza Smith (twenty-nine) the cook.

Joseph Crawhall was influenced by hereditary factors. An old Northumbrian family whose lineage can be traced back hundreds of years, the Crawhalls seem always to have been in a position of wealth. In a letter discussing the family crest Crawhall's father writes, 'the family appears to have been loafing about this country anytime these five hundred years. . . .'[4] In *Leges Marchiarum* or *Border-Laws* by William, Lord Bishop of Carlisle, it is recorded that the 'first distinct mention is found in *Novarum Inquisitiones* for 1340, where William Crawhall and John, son of William, are appointed commissioners of the Parish of Halt-whistle to levy the ninth of corn, wool and lamb for the crown.'[5] An early family home is recorded in Hodgson's *History of Northumberland*: 'Craw Hall, situated on a rock on the margin of the Tyne near its junction with the Allen, about five miles east of Haltwhistle, and opposite Ridley Hall, was an old residence of the Crawhalls and other families.' The walls and certain medieval architectural relics are said to remain.[6]

By the eighteenth century the Crawhalls were a prominent family in Newcastle. The artist's grandfather, Joseph Crawhall (1793–1853), is of importance in any study of Joseph junior. Renowned in his lifetime as a man of culture, he was also a keen sportsman and it is from him that Joseph inherited a love of hunting and an interest in the medium of watercolour.

Joseph Crawhall I was apprenticed in 1809 to Alderman Smith of St Peter's near Newcastle upon Tyne as a rope-maker. In 1812 he founded the firm of Joseph Crawhall, later Joseph Crawhall and Sons, at City Road, Newcastle upon Tyne, purchasing St Anne's Ropery, one of the most important factories in the north of England. In a history of the wire rope business he is described as 'a man of great good taste and creative talent in the realm of fine art . . .' and it is pointed out that such taste manifested itself in a notable feature of his factory – a chimney, built of stonework in the form of a rope.[7] The factory itself was seen as a 'landmark of new industrial enterprise.'[8]

Crawhall I played a prominent role in local affairs and was, in succession, Sheriff, Mayor (1849–50) and Alderman of Newcastle. He took a keen interest in politics, and loved entertaining, especially when in public office. He was described in 1836 as 'thoughtful, cautious, indefatigable and persevering. . . a keen observer of character and events' who took 'delight in mischief, but always has a reason for being mischievous.' He was one of those responsible for promoting the construction of the high-level bridge, and owned shares in various companies, including the Brompton Brewery and the Rotherhope Mine, and in coal. At the age of thirty-three, in 1826, Crawhall I is documented as being worth the considerable sum of £40,000.[9]

Esteemed as a generous supporter of charitable causes, Crawhall was also a founder member of the Northumberland Institution for the Promotion of Fine

Arts in the North of England, exhibiting at its first exhibition in 1822. In Havelock's *Local Records* he is described as 'a man of fine culture' who 'filled up a good deal of his leisure time in painting, chiefly in watercolour. The talents of Mr Crawhall as an artist were of so high an order as to warrant the belief that, if circumstances had led to his giving up the whole of his time to the brush, he would have achieved eminence.'[10]

Unfortunately insufficient pictorial evidence survives for us to judge the accuracy of this statement – though it is known that he covered his diaries and account books with pictorial records. One can, however, gain an idea of his watercolour style from a small volume bound with green leather containing handwritten records of the constitution and meetings of the Park House Club, dedicated to field-sports. The signatories to the Constitution of 22 October 1829 included George, William and Isaac Crawhall, Thomas Wilson, Joseph Obadiah Emerson, William Walton and a Mr Johnson. It is noticeable that in the listings of President and Vice-President the name Crawhall constantly appears.[11]

In the book the ink jottings list the days when the Club assembled and who was present, and itemise the catch. These notes are often prefaced with an ink and watercolour head-piece sketch depicting hare, grouse or pointer – whatever was most appropriate for the meet concerned. These head-pieces are very much in the style of Thomas Bewick with the animal shown in profile and the background vaguely indicated (pl 2). The drawing style is certainly adequate, though both the composition and the use of colour betray the hand of an amateur, albeit a competent one. A good example of his ability, and his defects, can be seen in the head-piece for Tuesday, 15 November 1831 (pl 3).

The bag usually consisted of hares, rabbits, grouse, pheasants, partridges, snipe and corncrakes. The meets sometimes lasted for as long as a week and the dedicated huntsmen would venture forth whatever the weather conditions. On one Tuesday it is recorded that 'weather very wet – that would have damped the ardour of any but genuine sportsmen, but did not deter the members from taking the Field nor spoilt the scent for the hounds, Four Hares being the reward of their skill and perseverance.'

The sense of humour, so evident in the work of Crawhall II and Crawhall III is very much in evidence here: the meeting of 22 May 1833 being illustrated with a scene showing a deserted hill-top with four members, one of whom, presumably the President, is perched on a very high rock above the others. It is the meetings of this club that are commemorated in Crawhall I's *Grouse Shooting Made Quite Easy to Every Capacity*, published in 1827 under the pseudonym, Jeffrey Gorcock. The book is illustrated with burlesques of the grouse-shooting incidents of the Club and with scenes of conviviality – food and drink, it seems, played an important role and one illustration depicts the men of the family – Emersons, Crawhalls and Bainbridges – sitting drinking, probably whisky.

Crawhall I's three surviving sons, Thomas Emerson (1819–92), Joseph (1821–

96) and George Edward (1833–1908), entered their father's rope-making firm as young men. The firm strove to remain in the forefront of technology, exhibiting one of Crawhall I's rope-making inventions at the Great Exhibition of 1851, referred to in the press as 'the most perfect thing of its kind yet invented.' A number of letters from Crawhall I to his wife recount his experiences at the exhibition, his delight in the interest shown in his invention and his excitement at the prospect of winning a prize after his years of endeavour.[12]

In 1887 at the Royal Mining, Engineering and Industrial Exhibition in Newcastle, the firm exhibited a patent plough stell flat rope, 480 yards long, 3 inches broad, ⅝ of an inch thick, with wire $^{100}/_{120}$ which attracted much attention. Soon afterwards, however, the firm passed out of the control of the Crawhall family, though whether the brothers sold the concern outright or retained some interest in it is not known. It has been suggested that the reason for the sale was a family feud, with George and Joseph joining forces against Thomas. But the firm continued to trade under the name of Crawhall, moving to premises in Gateshead in 1912.[13]

Joseph Crawhall II, the younger son, inherited his father's love of the fine arts (pl 4). One of the most fascinating personalities of the Victorian era, he was to play a vital role in the life and art of his son, Joseph. A late photograph portrays the elderly bearded gentleman seated at the huge desk in his study in Ealing surrounded by his beloved pictures, prints, porcelain and rare books (pl 6). A lifelong collector and antiquary, his field of collecting was wide, ranging from Neolithic flints to Jacobean armour and memorabilia of the '45, from ancient clay pipes to porcelain. He had a collection of books from the sixteenth century and an extensive collection of chapbooks and early treatises on angling.[14]

Unlike his father he was not interested in the hunt or in horses and, despite his love of angling, does not seem to have enjoyed living in the country. In a letter to his daughter Elspeth, then resident in London, written from his holiday base of Rothbury on 12 September 1885, he says 'living in such a dull place as this any tidings of loved friends are highly appreciated. I cannot say I enjoy it, I'm such a thoroughly confirmed town bird.'[15]

Crawhall II was born in West House, Newcastle, in what was at that time a prosperous part of the city. Despite his love for city living, he was not interested in politics and today he is known for the many books of sporting and antiquarian character that he produced – books which now have great value as collector's pieces. His first book, *The Compleatest Angling Booke that euer was Writ*, he wrote, illustrated and printed himself in Morpeth in 1859. This was the first of some seventeen books published by Crawhall between 1859 and 1889. These were all profusely illustrated with archaic woodcuts which Crawhall called 'sculptures'. Some of the books were hand-printed and then coloured by hand, and the broad use of yellows, reds and greens gives a jewel-like effect.

It is clear from the manuscript copies that survive – particularly those in Newcastle Public Library – just how many of Crawhall's own ideas went into the production and design of these books even when published by commercial printers. The type is chosen for its heavy and clumsy appearance – suited to the old spelling – and Crawhall's sense of design and *mise-en-page* is unerring. Even the briefest perusal of these books demonstrates the influence of the father on the son's use of line and washes of colour – though the end result is so very different.

Various members of the Crawhall family contributed illustrations to the first edition of *The Compleatest Angling Booke*, including his brother George who provided the tail-piece of a trout diving back into the water as 'The End'. From the manuscript copy we know that other contributors were his brother Thomas, sister Mary Elizabeth and a William Chapman. Crawhall's illustrations were sometimes recut from older designs and he was much influenced by Newcastle chapbooks of the period 1750–1850. The wood used for the printmaking was strong and blocky, thereby providing powerful expressive effects. Because *The Compleatest Angling Booke* was privately printed, only forty copies being produced, it is difficult to know how it was received by the public. Crawhall's *Newcastle Fisher's Garlands* of 1864, published by a commercial printer, did not receive favourable reviews. The critic from *The Athenaeum* talked of the 'uncouthness of the woodcuts, tail pieces,' saying that 'all . . . that stands for decoration is nothing short of sheer foppery.'[16]

Humour is one of the most important ingredients in the chapbook format and Crawhall's private jokes, at the expense of himself and his family, abound. There is, however, frequently a dichotomy between the text and the illustrations: 'it is part of Crawhall's technique of comic expressionism to body forth in many of his cuts sly innuendos or commentaries which show a tone quite different from the soberer words of many of the works that he illustrates.'[17] Genial good humour and a sense of fun are the cornerstone of Crawhall II's art and writing, qualities inherited by his artist son who, by 1880, would also be a contributor.

Joseph Crawhall II married Margaret Boyd, a Scot, in November 1854. That theirs was a happy marriage is clear from the many private jokes contained in his books and from the personal copies inscribed to her. In September 1885 he writes to his newly married daughter Elspeth, 'I'm delighted to think you've got so nicely and happily settled down in life. Mother and I've been "tuting" on about thirty-one years and happily.'[18]

It has been stated that Mrs Crawhall 'was distinguished less for ability in the arts, than for her success in the domestic sphere.' One of her daughters, however, wrote that 'she was much interested in art and helped Joe[III] in every way. She tried to make him work regularly, but it was not a success – she was always afraid of dying before Joe as he had almost always been with her, but she outlived him by several years – he died in 1913. She in 1928. She had great social gifts as well as a good housekeeper and in her youth was very handsome.'[19] Indeed, it was because of the devoted care of his mother and of his sister Beatrice, that Crawhall III could continue to work in the last years of his life.

Joseph had one brother, Hugh, and three sisters – Elspeth, Judith and Beatrice. From inscriptions and poems in family scrapbooks, and from family letters, it is clear that they were a happy, loving household. Many family jokes found their way into their father's books: Elspeth being the inspiration behind the Old Aunt Elspa children's books. In 1869 when Joseph was eight the family moved, possibly for business reasons, from Morpeth to 12 Eldon Square in Newcastle. Joseph attended Dame Elmslie's day school but family legend has it that he had a '. . . flair for playing truant. Any circus was likely to occasion such an escapade, and when the great annual fair appeared on the Town Moor, he would leave home early in the morning with a cold lunch in his pocket and not reappear until most of the family were in bed.'[20]

The picturesque and historic market-town of Morpeth, fourteen miles north of Newcastle, on the river Wansbeck, was Joseph's home for his first eight years. Morpeth was the ideal early environment for an artist whose life was to be dedicated to capturing and communicating a love of animals in watercolour and gouache. It is worthy of note that he had chosen his subject-matter while still under the age of twenty. Unlike so many of his contemporaries, Crawhall was attracted neither to the anecdotal subjects beloved of the Victorians, nor to portraiture which was to become the major source of patronage for his fellow artists and close friends Edward Arthur Walton (1860–1922), James Guthrie (1859–1930) and John Lavery (1856–1941).

We know little of his early but formative years. Family legend recounts how Joseph would lie for hours in the fields observing animals, often to the detriment of his health. The Crawhall family had previously resided at Bow Villa, Morpeth, but by the time of the 1861 Census, the year of Joseph's birth, they occupied Wansbeck House, an eighteenth-century stone mansion with a battlemented arch, built on the site of a previous mansion, Bagpipe Hall (demolished c.1750). In 1870, after the Crawhall family had moved to Newcastle, Wansbeck House became a day and boarding school for young ladies, later the Morpeth Girls' High School, and is still in use today for educational purposes.[21]

Unlike many of his contemporaries, however, Joseph Crawhall was encouraged to pursue a career in the arts. The young artist was nurtured in an environment where a love of nature and sport, reading and writing, as well as drawing and painting, were practised not only by his immediate family but, as we have seen, by previous generations too. By 1873 he was attending a preparatory school in Harrogate run by a Dr Ward, where the art teacher was John Collingham Moore (brother of the artist Albert). Moore is reputed to have said of Joseph, 'I can teach him nothing; he already knows more than I do.'[22]

From what we know of his home environment—surrounded by his father's collection and a witness to his father's creativity – it would seem that Joseph's artistic inclinations were encouraged. According to family legend Crawhall senior was much involved with the bringing up of his children. If the anecdotes are true,

4
Anonymous
Joseph Crawhall (1821–96)
c.1894
Carte-de-visite photograph
Scottish National Portrait
Gallery, Edinburgh

5
Joseph Crawhall (1821–96)
Cartoon
c.1879
Wash on paper, 17.5×12.0
Glasgow Art Gallery and
Museum

Chorus, from first Class Carriage:- "No room here - we're full!"
Inebriate (who has dined)" So am I!" "Tho'm I!"

6
Anonymous
Joseph Crawhall (1821–96)
c.1894
Photograph
Central Library, Newcastle
upon Tyne

of his taking young Joseph fishing and to the circus, then he was directly responsible for influencing young Joseph's choice of subject-matter. It is amusing to observe that in his *Album of Ideas for Adverts* he notes that he will try his hand at 'any subject except horses'[23] – his son made horses one of his main specialities.

Crawhall II obviously did not insist that any of his children follow him into business. Hugh never settled on a career although he did try his hand at pioneering in Nebraska. Beatrice, the youngest, another city-lover, had a strong interest in the theatre. It has been suggested that Oscar Wilde courted her. It can be no coincidence that one of Crawhall senior's commonplace books contains various press-cuttings relating to Wilde. Any liaison, however, was not encouraged and a family scrapbook of 1883–4 includes verses that prove that Wilde had become *persona non grata* in the household. Later letters suggest that the friendship was resumed but at a distance. In a letter, written in 1885, Oscar Wilde writes to Crawhall II at 2 Sydenham Terrace, Newcastle, 'Dear Mr Crawhall, The Directory is right for once – my address is 16 Tite Street: I was quite disappointed to miss you last Monday: but am glad to hear you have more marvels in store for the public. With kind regards to your wife and daughters, very truly yours, Oscar Wilde.'[24]

There may have been a stronger bond between Crawhall and Joseph than between other members of the family because of their shared love of art. It would appear that the rest of the family did not take Crawhall senior's art too seriously – Beatrice and Mrs Crawhall seemingly continually complaining that too much money was spent on his hobbies, including the publication of books.

Crawhall senior's lively sense of humour is very much in evidence in a series of nineteen scrapbooks, full of cartoons inspired by direct observation of everyday situations.[25] It was these cartoons – these very books in fact – that Crawhall lent to Charles Keene for use for *Punch* (pl 5). It is not known when Crawhall began doing these cartoons or even for what reason, but they are an amusing social document of the time, demonstrating his inexhaustible sense of fun and his capacity to capture the character of human types of all classes. Keene's biographer noted that, sometime prior to 1872, 'Mr. Crawhall, ever a lover of things quaint, grotesque, and jocular, had been in the habit of jotting down any telling incident he might hear of or observe, illustrating it at leisure in colours for his own amusement.'[26]

Charles Keene (1823–91) is one of the most original of all British draughtsmen and was certainly one of the great artists of the nineteenth century. Keene was probably introduced to Crawhall in 1872 and within a few years the two men had become intimate friends with a common interest in music, pipes (smoking and musical) and antiquarianism. Crawhall's book *Border Notes*, 1880, is dedicated to Keene.

The extensive correspondence from Keene to Crawhall provided the foundation for Layard's biography of Keene, and it is a great pity that the corresponding letters from Crawhall were not preserved for they would certainly have shed light on the early career of Joseph junior. Layard estimated that approximately two hundred and fifty cartoons by Crawhall were used by Keene in the pages of *Punch*. These were published between 1877 and 1890 – the last cartoon being that for *At The Zoo* published in *Punch* on 5 April 1890. In return Keene sent Crawhall many of his original *Punch* sketches. Keene acknowledged the debt he owed to Crawhall. In a letter of 24 May 1878 Keene writes, 'I shall be very glad to take advantage of your kind offer of some more sketch-books. I'm sending you two that I have, from which I've extracted the honey.'[27] Keene most certainly benefited from Crawhall's sense of humour. One contemporary recounts how friends 'of the late Charles Keene were frequently led to remark on his lack of humour in conversation. How did it come about that he was always pawky and entertaining in the pages of *Punch*?'[28]

Crawhall's humour, however, was sometimes too broad for *Punch* – 'The gathering smog of Victorian prudery had little effect on Crawhall.'[29] In a letter of 28 September 1878, Keene writes, 'You will have noticed that our sapient editor took all the fun out of your subject of the Undertaker and the uncanny customer. I complained about it . . .'[30]

The relationship between the two men is important for our purposes in that it is in these letters that we learn of the progress of young Joseph. In a letter to Crawhall of 22 June 1877 Keene writes, 'let me know at what time you will be in London this autumn, when you bring your lad to the university. Have you settled on his domicile? When I mentioned about this to my friend Haydon, he asked me if I thought he was a studious lad (Haydon has a son who goes to King's College), as he would like to take and board him, and the two boys could study together of an evening. He lives in a beautiful house in the grounds at Bethlehem Hospital, Southwark (but quite detached). I fancy he would be very comfortable there, but you will judge best. I also have a friend who lives in Gower Street, close to University College, an artist, Davis Cooper, the son of old Abraham Cooper, R.A. I know he has often pupils who live in his house, but perhaps while the lad is studying it would be better he was apart from art distraction . . . if I can help you beforehand in any way in this matter, command me. . . .'[31]

Crawhall did not avail himself of his friend's help. Joseph was enrolled at King's College School in the Strand in May 1877, and when the school year began in September he boarded with a Mr E. Brooksmith, 28 Tregunter Grove, South Kensington. Crawhall evidently agreed with Keene that too much 'art distraction' would not be good for his son, for Keene in his next letter says, 'I think you are right in not wishing your boy to be diverted in the Art direction yet.'[32]

This did not mean that young Joseph was not continuing with his art studies. He went on to win Middle School drawing prizes for the Lent and Summer terms in 1878 and 1879. It has even been suggested that Joseph had already found a market for drawings of a semi-humorous sporting character while still at school.[33] Keene was aware of the type of subject-matter that attracted Joseph because in 1878 he writes of an incident involving cricketers and an uninvited bull-terrier. 'You might like this for your scrap-book, and your animal painter could do the dog.'[34] Later the same year he writes 'Kindest regards to Mrs Crawhall and all your sons and daughters. I hope the coming Landseer has sold his picture.'[35]

Joseph's health, a perpetual problem, is discussed in Keene's letter of 16 December 1878: 'I hope your son is better. Lawson told me he had got a chill and severe cold from sitting in wet clothes, but we hoped, from your not mentioning it, that he was getting over it. Hammer it into the boy's mind that he may overeat, get drunk, act any imprudence, except that, till he's forty; by that time he'll know it himself.'[36] Keene's enquiries continued throughout the following year: 'How does your son get on with his work – the artist?' 'How does your son the painter get on? I suppose he'll be sending to the R.A. next year.'[37]

A valuable indication of Joseph's self-critical appraisal of his own work comes in a letter of 16 July 1880. 'How does Joe get on with his painting? That disposition he seems to have of getting dissatisfied with his work shows he's a real artist, but try and get him to stick hard to his ideas and work 'em out to the bitter end! – the end will perhaps be bitter for some time, but it must be swallowed. You'll have to make him realise by keeping him short of money! Did he carry out that picture of the Shepherd and his Dog in the Highland Cottage?'[38]

Keene's interest in the young artist continued, for in June 1881 he says, 'Let me know if Joe is in town, and if he is at the same address.' Crawhall is obviously keeping Keene apprised of the exhibitions that Joseph is represented at, for the following year Keene asks, 'What is Joe doing – has he sold?' and in 1883, informing his friend that he has been asked to the Royal Academy dinner again (by the Aberdeen granite manufacturer and collector, Alexander Macdonald), he comments, 'I hope Joe has sent to the Academy, though there's rather a terrible trio of hangers this year.' That year was the only one in which a work by Joseph, *A Lincolnshire Pasture* (pl 22), was hung.[39]

After this period their correspondence dwindles. In a letter to his sister Mary in 1889 Crawhall II writes of their feeling of isolation, in their large house at 2 Sydenham Terrace in Newcastle, and he speaks of the possibility 'of leaving the north and settling possibly in London as I have a lot of nice friends there such as Lawson, Keene etc., and my house is now really so large for three of us.'[40] By June 1890 they were installed at 21 Castle Bar Road, Ealing – close to their eldest daughter Elspeth and her family.

Keene and Crawhall shared a love of the prints and publications of the great draughtsman and artist-craftsman Thomas Bewick (1753–1828) who is mentioned frequently in their letters. This is of particular interest for the light it sheds on Joseph's training in art. Every writer – both contemporary and recent – commenting on Joseph's early training, records that his father insisted he work from memory rather than directly from nature, and that he was not allowed to

7
The Fieldfare
c.1875
Pencil on paper, 14.7×16.5
The Burrell Collection

correct the memorised works. Joseph was encouraged to observe, for hours if necessary, and to draw only things that he knew. This accords with what we know of Crawhall's father's own technique as he frequently cut directly on to the block from memory, often without having made a preparatory drawing.

Crawhall III's friend, the artist Sir John Lavery, insisted that Joseph never used a sketchbook or worked direct from nature. Sufficient sketchbook studies exist to prove otherwise but it seems likely that normally he did work from memory rather than from nature. Unlike young Joseph, Charles Keene is known to have drawn directly from nature – his 'humour was the humour of observation rather than the humour of invention.'[41] Crawhall II did not begin by insisting on the use of memory alone. Young Joseph would have been encouraged to sift through his father's collection of prints and drawings and work from them. The juvenilia that survive are mainly of animal subjects copied from Thomas Bewick.

Brought up in the countryside in Northumberland, Bewick specialised in the depiction of birds and domestic and farm animals. What delighted Bewick was producing humorous head- and tail-pieces and the backgrounds for his studies rather than the full studies of birds and animals. This was in contrast to Joseph. A series of Joseph's drawings dating from the period 1873–5 demonstrates that his subject-matter was already selected (at the tender age of eleven) – donkeys, cows, stags, dogs and birds. The drawings had been lovingly pasted into one of Crawhall's family albums. *The Fieldfare* (pl 7) and *The Sparrow* are direct copies

8
*Thomas Bewick
(1753–1828)
The Chillingham Bull
1789
Wood-engraving*

9
*The Bull
March 1875
Pencil and chalk on paper,
12.8×22.7
The Burrell Collection*

10
*The Old Cow
c.1894–1903
Gouache on linen,
30.3×44.1
The Burrell Collection*

of Bewick's illustrations in his *A History of British Birds* while Joseph's *The Bull*
(pl 9), dated March 1875, is a copy of Bewick's famous *The Chillingham Bull*
(pl 8). Many years later the image was to reappear in his *The Old Cow* (pl 10).

There were various links between the Bewick and the Crawhall families – for
Crawhall's links with the Bewick heritage were much stronger than merely
possessing books and prints. Crawhall II was one of the executors of the will of
Thomas's daughter, Isabella Bewick, for which he received a legacy of £90. It was
Crawhall, too, who inherited Bewick's tool box and who prepared the catalogue
for the sale of the Bewick effects in Newcastle in 1884. One of the items in the sale
suggests that the Crawhall–Bewick link goes back to an earlier generation. Indeed
Thomas Bewick is known to have said of Crawhall I that 'Joseph . . . excelled as a
painter, for which nature had furnished him with the requisite innate powers – but
in this he was taken off by his business of a Rope maker.'[42] This item was a
Northumberland election caricature of 1826 by Crawhall I given to 'Mr. Bewick,
with Joseph Crawhall's com'ts.' It is also possible that Crawhall II might have
learned to engrave on wood from one of Bewick's many students.

Crawhall II was interested in bringing culture and art to Newcastle. His
public-mindedness is already evident in his books. As his biographer noted, one 'of
the most refreshing aspects of Crawhall's artistic genius is his recognition that art
should do more than simply fill expensive books or be hung on elegant walls. His
"texts" show that he has an awareness of art's role for a broader public.'[43] This
concern is further seen in his involvement in the founding and running of the Arts

Association of Newcastle. From his scrapbooks and from his own commonplace book we can see that he played a major role in the setting up, selecting and hanging of these exhibitions.

From 1878 he was joint secretary with Cartmell Ridley and from 1880 he acted as secretary alone. They arranged biennial exhibitions, frequent conversaziones and even the occasional ball. The aims of the Association were to promote a taste for art and to encourage local art, and it was hoped that sufficient funds would eventually lead to the establishment of a permanent art gallery in the town. Each contributor was permitted a maximum of three works, none of which could have been previously exhibited in Newcastle.

By 1877 Crawhall had contacted most of the prominent artists of the day and had asked them to submit pictures for exhibition and possible sale. In terms of sales the exhibitions were a success: 133 works sold in 1878 fetching £4,026; 73 in 1879 for £2,376; and the two exhibitions in 1880, with 140 works sold, bringing in £6,293.[44]

In his letters Keene frequently asks about preparations for the exhibitions and suggests and recommends various artists. Keene also commiserates with Crawhall over his lack of a summer holiday, because of the work, albeit voluntary, involved. His commitment, however, was to affect his health in another way. A newspaper report in the *Newcastle Journal* of 2 September 1878 headed 'Disastrous Gas Explosion' shows just how far poor Crawhall had to go in the pursuit of his labour. 'Early on Saturday morning a disastrous explosion occurred at the Assembly Rooms . . . causing considerable destruction of property and personal injury to two persons, viz. Mr. Joseph Crawhall of Eldon Square, and a policeman named Jahez Darley.' Because of preparations for the forthcoming exhibition 'workmen are being employed adding new gas jets and fittings for hanging the pictures . . . and it is unfortunately in connection with the alterations now proceeding that the explosion occurred . . . One of the preparations is the addition to the reception room of a gas pipe running across the room and containing a large number of jets for the purpose of the proper illumination of the room in the evenings; the pipe had been placed and attached to the gas main, and the workmen were in some way still employed upon it, and it was left on Friday night, as was supposed all safe.' The report proceeds to relate in detail how the next morning when Crawhall and the policeman arrived and suspected a leakage of gas, Crawhall immediately opened one of the large windows but the policeman 'got a step ladder . . . placed it in the middle of the room, beneath the gas pipe, and mounting the ladder so as to be able to reach the taps, he proceeded to strike a match. While getting out the match, Mr Crawhall, who was then standing at the door leading from the reception room into the grand ball-room, asked the policeman if he thought it would be safe to strike a light; but the warning was unheeded, and the match was struck. A terrific explosion immediately followed. The policeman was blown off the steps and fell to the floor insensible; and at the same time Mr Crawhall was knocked down and considerably injured. The doors and windows of the room were blown out with great violence . . . a large number of works of art . . . were found to have been thrown down and injured . . .' However, the brunt of the explosion was felt in the watercolour room, 'the least valuable portion of the collection'. The report goes on to say that the 'money value of the collection amounts to fifty or sixty thousand pounds, and is insured for £40,000 in the North British Insurance Office.' It continues, 'Mr Crawhall received a severe shock and was very much scorched about the face and hands, and his clothes were destroyed.' Crawhall was not sufficiently recovered to attend the exhibition opening, but in the many speeches recorded he was warmly thanked for his valuable contribution to the preparations.

A review in the *Newcastle Chronicle* at the end of the exhibition, of 18 November, claims that 'Art, except at the Academy, is never a very great draw. One does not expect to see as many people at an exhibition of pictures as at a circus on a big night.' The reviewer concedes that the exhibition had been a financial success. It was at these Newcastle exhibitions that young Joseph made his début as an artist/exhibitor. In the 1878 exhibition he exhibited two works, probably oils: *Fox-Hounds, Morpeth* and *A Collie Dog. The Fox Terrier* (pl 11), from the following year, gives a clear indication of the young artist's ability. His contribution went further as a number of the line drawings in the *Exhibition Notes* were by him.

Joseph's work *Fox-Hounds* is illustrated in the *Exhibition Notes* and is commented on as being 'lifelike and animated'. From the illustration, *Fox-Hounds* would appear to have been very close in style to the early drawings mentioned above and owing much to Bewick. Crawhall II compiled the exhibition catalogue, which contains some of Bewick's illustrations, printed from the original blocks, lent by Miss Bewick. A reviewer in the *Newcastle Chronicle* of 7 September 1878 writes that the 'work of Mr J. Crawhall, jun., is much better than the work of the ordinary amateur. His *Fox-hounds* are well and carefully painted, whilst the *Collie Dog* is a finished little picture, despite its simplicity.'

In the Preface to the notes, one of the editors, William De Brailsford, writes about the growing interest in the arts and the exhibitions in 'Liverpool, Manchester, Edinburgh and Glasgow' which 'have each and all come to the fore and manifested a sense of the requirements of the age. Is Newcastle to be content with exclusion from the realms of art? . . . the promoters of the Fine Arts Association, this day inaugurated, appeal to the good taste of their fellow-townsmen, and seek their co-operation in an undertaking which has had for its basis the laudable desire to spread a love for the beautiful amongst us.'

In the autumn exhibition of the following year Joseph submitted the maximum number of works and all three were accepted; priced between £10 and £12, the subjects were again animals. It is at this exhibition that his artist friend from Glasgow, E. A. Walton, was also represented.[45] In the *Notes on the Principle*

Pictures prepared for the 1879 exhibition, it is said that although some of the 'big' names (e.g. Orchardson and Watts) are no longer here 'The quality of the works exhibited is more even, and the general tone is of higher character. Selectors have been more rigorous and as a result some young local artists haven't done so well.' The *Notes* end with comment that a 'young painter of high promise, Mr. Crawhall jun., exhibits several clever animal studies, which prove that he has chosen a line of work admirably suited to his talent.'

In the 1880 spring loan and sale exhibition Crawhall II was a major lender in the prints and porcelain section. He lent prints after Parmigianino, Mantegna, Marc-Antonio Raimondi, Schongauer and Dürer, and etchings by Ostade and Both. He also lent many books. In a review of this exhibition it is claimed that one 'of the most important and interesting features of the exhibition is the rare and valuable collection of engravings of the old masters . . . which have been lent by the secretary, Mr Joseph Crawhall. . . . The members of the Association and the visitors to the exhibition have in this matter a special cause for gratitude to Mr Crawhall, who has not only lent his large collection of engravings, but has written in the catalogue a series of concise descriptions relating to the history and process of engraving itself and to the artists and character of the different schools which his engravings illustrate.'[46]

Joseph was again represented by three works: *Bolted* (executed with James Guthrie), *Drowsy* and *Calf (from life)*. The *Newcastle Chronicle*'s reviewer wrote that in *Bolted* 'Mr Guthrie, we believe, is responsible for the landscape, and Mr Crawhall for the man on horseback. The former although somewhat too rough for exhibition purposes, is good in colour and feeling; and the latter is very spirited, though not perfectly drawn.'[47]

Although Joseph's friends Guthrie and Walton exhibited three and two works respectively in the autumn exhibition, Joseph only exhibited one: *Sleeping Dog* at £6. Crawhall's last contribution was in the autumn of 1881 when his *Study of a Trout* and *A Caution* were exhibited. Although there is no suggestion that Joseph's works were only accepted because of his father's role on the committee, it is surely no coincidence that, in the year Crawhall II resigned from the committee Joseph ceased exhibiting at Newcastle.

There can be no doubting the importance of the influence of Crawhall II on Joseph. Joseph shared his father's sharpness of eye but had a defter hand. Crawhall II died at a temporary London home, 27 Kildare Terrace West, on 7 July 1896 – the many obituaries paying homage to the power of his personality, his influence and skill. Joseph Crawhall II was a man of great talent and originality who breathed new and abounding vitality into the art of the chapbook. Ever fertile in ideas, he had a broad humour and a caustic wit combined with a wonderful sense of pattern and acute powers of observation. The obituary in the *Newcastle Daily Journal* of 9 July 1896 says his death 'removes from the local life of the North of England one who has, in almost all spheres but the sphere of politics, been for many years past one of its most conspicuous and interesting figures.' It continues, 'Mr Crawhall was a genius . . . with activities diffused over innumerable fields. It was delightful to spend an hour or two in his company, among his exceedingly miscellaneous treasures. . . . Specifically he represented to our own generation the taste for the old chapbooks, the old broad-sheets, the old woodcuts hacked out with a knife.'[48]

11
The Fox Terrier
1879
Oil on canvas, 30.5×45.7
Private Collection

12
James Guthrie
Joseph Crawhall Seated
1881
Etching, 14.3×11.4
Glasgow Art Gallery and
Museum

CHAPTER

2

ONE OF THE BOYS

In an unpublished tribute, the Glasgow writer and artist Macaulay Stevenson claimed that Joseph Crawhall's 'pictures could never be mistaken for those of any other artist ... while others labour and blunder and stumble and perchance at length succeed in getting a sense of truth into their work, Crawhall, with but a few slight yet incisive touches, hits off the vital points to a nicety, and you feel that his terse, epigrammatic telling has left nothing more to be said.'[1] While one may agree with Stevenson about the uniqueness of his art, there are sound stylistic, geographical and personal reasons for classifying Crawhall with the Glasgow Boys.

How did the young Newcastle artist come into contact with his Glaswegian counterparts? We have already seen how Joseph's father had created the ideal environment for the encouragement and training of his artist son. Crawhall senior was equally to encourage and be encouraged by the endeavours of two young Scottish artists who were warmly welcomed into the Crawhall household. These young men, James Guthrie and E. A. Walton, were to become Joseph's lifelong friends. It is not known exactly how, or precisely when Joseph first met Guthrie and Walton. What is known is that in the later 1870s, Joseph's sister Judith was being courted by E. A. Walton's elder brother Richard (1855–1938). Richard had come to Newcastle to work as an insurance secretary and when Judith and

Richard married on 1 June 1881 Joseph was their best man. During the period of their courtship Joseph would have met E. A. Walton who would have impressed the young Newcastle artist with tales of his training and of the artistic climate in Glasgow. Many visits to Glasgow were to follow and during one of these, in 1878 or 1879, Joseph Crawhall was introduced to Guthrie.

Edward Arthur Walton (1860–1922), five years younger than his brother Richard, was the sixth son of the merchant, manufacturer and amateur artist Jackson Walton (d.1873). After a short period of formal academic art training at Düsseldorf Academy in Germany, Walton attended classes at the Glasgow School of Art. In 1877, with Guthrie, W. Y. Macgregor and James Paterson, Walton had applied for membership of the Glasgow Art Club but was rejected. Following his first exhibition at the Glasgow Institute of the Fine Arts in 1878 he was successfully elected to the club. Quiet, reticent, hard-working and good-natured, Walton quickly established a rapport with Crawhall. He attended St Mungo's Art Society and it was at one of their meetings that he met Guthrie. Later to win renown as one of the most distinguished of Scottish portraitists, James Guthrie (1859–1930) was the third son and fourth and youngest child of the Reverend John Guthrie. Quiet, tactful and diplomatic, Guthrie was described by the artist D. Y. Cameron as 'a man of strange and alluring personality, pure of heart, greatly gifted, greatly loved, and greatly honoured.'[2] Unlike Crawhall, Guthrie was not at first permitted to follow his artistic inclinations and studied law at the University of Glasgow. However he abandoned his studies and travelled to London in the summer of 1878 and, although he took a studio, he did not enrol as a student in the art academies or schools.

Although largely self-taught, Guthrie was influenced by one of the most successful Scottish artists working in London, John Pettie (1839–93). Crawhall, attending school in London during the winter of 1879, visited Guthrie at his studio in 2 Elgin Road and so both young artists 'benefitted from Pettie's comments on what they were doing and from visits to his studio, where they saw his pictures in course of being painted.'[3] Typically Victorian in his choice of anecdotal, sentimental subjects, Pettie was admired by the artists of the Glasgow school for his painterly qualities. Pettie's influence on the young Guthrie can be gauged even in the titles of early works such as *A Gallant of the Terror*, exhibited at the Newcastle Arts Association in the autumn of 1880.

That Crawhall and Guthrie were indeed close during this period is evident from Guthrie's painting, *An Unpublished Tragedy* (whereabouts unknown). The painting was an early work and appeared at auction at Christie's in 1924. One newspaper reported how the 'few pounds for which the big Pettie–Guthrie composition was sold to a London dealer proved, conclusively, that its interest was not generally discerned.'[4] The article describes the picture where in a dark interior three figures only half listen to an author reading his work. It has been suggested that one of the three figures, 'the young man seated beyond the table was painted from Crawhall . . .'[5] It is possible that Crawhall played a more important role in the gestation of the work, for there is the distinct possibility that the 'admirably painted dog' was from his hand. In a letter to Sir Frederick Gardiner, Guthrie said that he and Crawhall 'were always together at this time, and, although I can't remember this, he may have given me a hand with the dog.'[6] When the painting was rejected at the Royal Academy in 1881, Guthrie, at the suggestion of Crawhall's father, sent it to the Newcastle Arts Association where at a price of £110 it found a purchaser.[7] The painting was obviously of importance to Guthrie, for he purchased it back in 1924 to give to his son.

Although Pettie might have encouraged Guthrie to try etching, it is equally plausible and evidence exists to suggest that it was Crawhall's father who provided the motivating force. Guthrie's etching *Joe* (pl 12), exhibited at the Glasgow Institute of Fine Arts in the autumn of 1881, dates from the same period as Guthrie's and Crawhall's drawings for Crawhall senior's *The Compleatest Angling Booke*. Crawhall is depicted in the half light, smoking and pensive in a pose that might well have been influenced by Keene's etching *Grief*.[8] While one cannot be certain that Crawhall did collaborate with Guthrie in the painting of *An Unpublished Tragedy*, it is known that they worked together on *Bolted*, exhibited in 1880 at the Newcastle Arts Association and on one of the drawings for *The Compleatest Angling Booke* (pl 91).[9] Their collaboration and friendship took various forms and Walton, when back in Glasgow, kept in touch by letter and joined his two friends in exhibiting at the Newcastle Arts Association – all three encouraged, no doubt, by Crawhall's father.

During the summers from 1879 until 1890 Crawhall, Guthrie and Walton worked together, and often with other artists of the Glasgow school, at Rosneath on the river Clyde, Brig o'Turk in the Trossachs, Crowland in Lincolnshire, Cockburnspath in Berwickshire and at Cambuskenneth near Stirling. One of the most important factors in the development of the art of all three was the companionship of these shared painting trips – their intimacy and conviviality were recorded in their drawings and photographs of the period. After a day working outside from nature they would gather together in the evening. Not one of the three was given to making intellectual pronouncements about art and even Guthrie, who was well-read and able to communicate, seldom talked about his painting. Together, though, they discussed their aims, the artists they admired and future exhibitions. Despite the rather seedy scene of drunkenness implied in Guthrie's caricature (pl 13), none of them was particularly flamboyant or reckless. Guthrie's ink sketch might well have been inspired by a similar scene in *The Compleatest Angling Booke*, showing Crawhall's father and his brothers, Thomas and George (pl 14). It was during such evenings that Walton, Guthrie and Crawhall played the game of 'Heads, bodies and legs' (pls 15, 16). These draw-ings, which had been folded as in the game of consequences, usually portrayed a local character. 'Guthrie would begin on the top third with the head and shoulders, Joe would draw the trunk and thighs on the centre piece and Walton would attempt the legs and feet on what remained. In this order, but in no other, the combination made for pictorial balance.'[10] One can imagine them giggling over the day's events, including an episode that, no doubt through Crawhall's father, found its way into *Punch's Almanack* for 1880. The boys had been making fun of an itinerant preacher who retorted, 'Ah twig ye ahint the stanes there, laddies – smockin-but ye may smock-an' ye may smock-an' ye may smock – but ye'll smock faur sairer whaur ye're gaun tae.' The dialect unfortunately was toned down in print.[11] Another important aspect of this companionship was mutual support and encouragement. Although we know of no period in his life when Crawhall himself suffered from dejection, his friends did experience crises of confidence. In a letter to John Lavery, Guthrie portrays himself as a round-eyed, woeful artist, hands to head in pained anguish (pl 17). He writes, 'Sure as death John I am useless rubbish and can go nowhere except to the mischief. Things are all wrong with me – I'm in the worst Prussian blues I have ever had.'[12]

In the autumn of 1882 Crawhall travelled to Paris and enrolled in the atelier of Aimé Morot (1850–1913). Guthrie had visited Paris a few months earlier and no doubt encouraged his friend, who lacked confidence in the handling of oil, to seek formal training. A letter to Walton of 1880 suggests that Crawhall's father,

13
James Guthrie
Caricature of Walton,
Guthrie and Crawhall
c.1882–4
Ink on paper, 8.3×11.3
Scottish National Portrait
Gallery, Edinburgh

14
Illustration in Joseph
Crawhall's Compleatest
Angling Booke, *2nd ed. 1881*

15
E. A. Walton, James Guthrie
and Joseph Crawhall
*Game of Heads, Bodies and
Legs*
c.1882–4
Pencil on paper, 22.5×15.8
*National Gallery of Scotland,
Edinburgh*

16
E. A. Walton, James Guthrie
and Joseph Crawhall
*Game of Heads, Bodies and
Legs*
c.1882–4
Pencil on paper, 17.5×11.6
*National Gallery of Scotland,
Edinburgh*

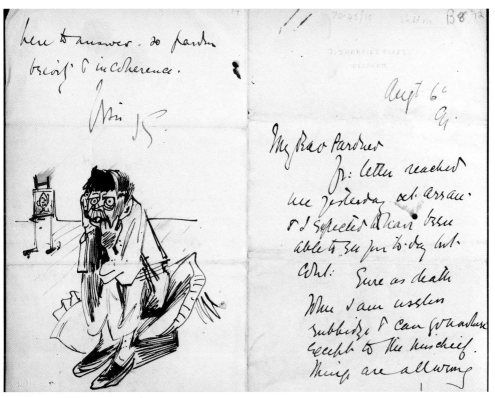

17
James Guthrie
Letter to John Lavery
1899
Tate Archives, London

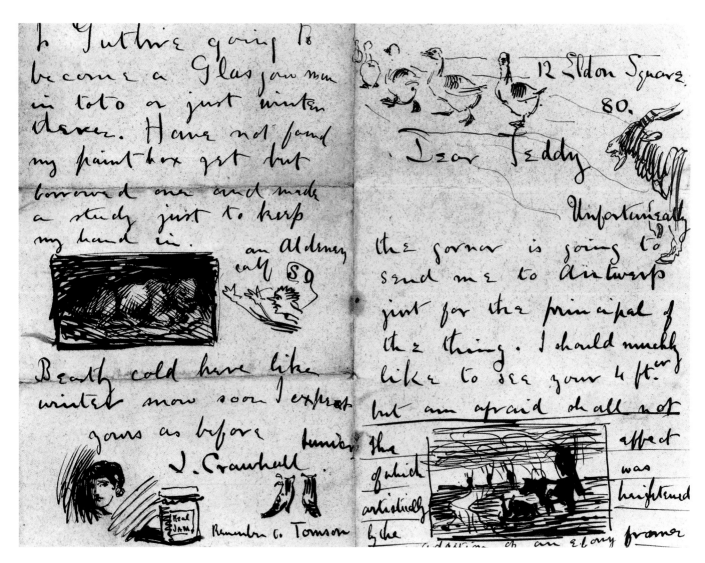

18
Letter to E. A. Walton
1880
Ink on light blue paper,
17.6 × 22.6
National Gallery of Scotland,
Edinburgh

himself aware of his son's lack of experience in this field, had already tried to persuade him to study abroad (pl 18)[13]. Crawhall writes, 'Dear Teddy, Unfortunately the guvnor is going to send me to Antwerp just for the principal of the thing. I should muchly like to see your 4fter, but am afraid shall not . . . Is Guthrie going to become a Glasgow man in toto or just winter there. Have not found my paintbox yet but borrowed one and made a study just to keep my hand in. . . . Beastly cold here like winter snow soon I expect, yours as before, J. Crawhall Junior.' There is, however, no evidence to confirm that the letter actually refers to the Antwerp Academy, nor that Crawhall ever studied there.

Opinions vary as to the importance of Crawhall's visit to Paris. While his experience there might have contributed to his growing dissatisfaction with oil as a medium, it was not instrumental in influencing his move to watercolour. This change came about within the next few years as a result of his first visit to Tangier. Some contemporaries insist that Crawhall learnt nothing during his stay in Paris.

It is certainly difficult to imagine him submitting to the routine of the studio and being forced to work directly from a model. Although he only remained there for two months, pictorial evidence does suggest that his palette lightened, his compositions became more rigorously structured and his brushstrokes more controlled. A comparison of *The Milkmaid* (pl 19) and *A Lincolnshire Stream* (pl 20), both of 1882, demonstrates this change quite clearly. Dating from before the Paris trip, *The Milkmaid* emphasises tonal values rather than colour and drawing. In *A Lincolnshire Stream* the brushstrokes are applied with a new confidence. The composition is strongly conceived and the dark tones carefully balanced – elements, however, that could have been learned as much from his Glasgow Boy friends as from his Paris experience. Unfortunately there are no securely documented works from Crawhall's stay in Paris. The *French Cab Horse* (pl 21), while certainly a Parisian subject, may have been executed during a later visit to the city or may even have been worked from memory after the trip of 1882.

The choice of Aimé Morot's atelier was an interesting and no doubt carefully

19
The Milkmaid
1882
Oil on panel, 15.5×20.5
Sir Norman and Lady
Macfarlane

considered one. Morot, like Crawhall's father, was known to stress the importance of memory. In addition, he loved painting animals, especially horses, gaining
fame for his spirited cavalry pieces. Morot had won the coveted Prix-de-Rome in
1873 and after 1880 travelled extensively in Morocco, Spain and the Sudan. If
Crawhall had studied his later pictures, it is possible he may have been influenced
by his colourful renditions of the Spanish bullfight, *Toro Collante* (1883) and
Bravo Toro (1884). Throughout the 1880s Morot painted 'pompier' works of
nudes in forests or seductresses with snakes, very much in the manner of
Bouguereau and not the type of work that would have appealed to Crawhall or
artists of the Glasgow school. Subsequently renowned as a portraitist Morot was
reputedly in Spain throughout Crawhall's time at his atelier and this might
account for the young artist's cavalier attitude to his studies. In his autobiography
A. S. Hartrick (1864–1950) recalls meeting Crawhall 'in Paris, where he was
living at the same hotel as myself. He never went to work in any atelier there that I
can remember, though he had entered one under Aimé Morot . . . but wandered
about les Halles, the great market there, where he found subjects that suited him. I
think he only completed one drawing in Paris – that of a bull – but he was always
tearing up what he had done if it did not achieve what he was after. It is a curious
fact, I remember, that his favourite work in the Louvre was Courbet's "Man with
a Leathern Belt".'[14]

On his return from Paris Crawhall joined Guthrie and Walton at Crowland in
Lincolnshire. Here they eagerly discussed contemporary French art and deplored
the work of the contemporary British school. They, in common with the other
Glasgow Boys, disliked the panoramic landscape views then so popular and
deplored the 'literary' emphasis on incident and anecdote in most Victorian
painting. They were interested in 'painterly' concerns – problems of pictorial
representation, harmonious design and unity – and not with the 'finish' and 'fact'
of their academic contemporaries. Like the academic artists, the Glasgow Boys
looked to, and worked directly from, nature but it was what they made of this that
was to mark them out as different: 'The new men went to nature, not to catalogue
or classify, but to select, interpret and clarify.'[15]

It is important to pause to consider the nature of the influence of contemporary
French and Dutch art on the work of Crawhall and to relate this to Glasgow's role
at the end of the nineteenth century as an internationally important and innovative
artistic centre. The second city of the Empire, Glasgow's industries – shipbuilding,
the machine industry, the production of coal, iron and eventually steel – were to
create a climate of confidence and a prosperity that resulted in widespread
patronage of the arts. The founding of the Fine Art Institute in 1861 (later the
Royal Glasgow Institute of the Fine Arts) and, in 1867, of the Glasgow Art Club
provided an outlet for the sale of contemporary works. These institutions also
offered the opportunity for young artists to view important loan exhibitions of
works by the Barbizons (Millet, Rousseau and Diaz), Bastien-Lepage and artists of

20
A Lincolnshire Stream
1882
Oil on canvas, 32.2×22.3
Cecil Higgins Art Gallery,
Bedford

21
French Cab Horse
c.1882–92
Watercolour heightened with
bodycolour on paper,
30.0×43.5
Private Collection

22
A Lincolnshire Pasture
1883
Oil on canvas, 91.4×127
Dundee Art Galleries and
Museum

23
Landscape with Cattle
c.1883–5
Oil on canvas, 43.0×57.8
Glasgow Art Gallery and
Museum

the Hague school (Israels, Mauve and the brothers Maris). Such works could also be viewed in the galleries of dealers like Craibe Angus and Alexander Reid, who in the 1880s found a ready sale for such works to prosperous Scottish industrialists like W. A. Coats, Leonard Gow and William Burrell. This artistic activity was a new phenomenon. In 1888 a reviewer commented, 'To those who can recollect the condition of Glasgow some twenty years ago, the advance which has been made since then, both with regard to the production of works of art and their appreciation, must warrant reflection.'[16]

Whilst there were distinct differences in the styles of the Glasgow Boys, they shared three basic tenets: a pursuit of true tonal relationships and values in colour; a belief that technical qualities were more important than the appeal of the subject; and a belief that the decorative element of design was fundamental. Their 'creed . . . was that a picture should be a work of art. Firstly and lastly its appeal should be to the aesthetic sense, and based on form, colour, or tone . . . They were not content with the appeal of romance or sentiment or even the impressionism which was a loyal record of nature, unless these qualities were combined with decorative values which made the work a joy to the eye . . .'[17]

Crawhall's *A Lincolnshire Pasture* (pl 22) and *Landscape with Cattle* (pl 23) show how far he, like the other Glasgow Boys, was influenced by contemporary French and Dutch painting and both works bear all the hallmarks of these influences. The static composition, the choice of subject and the placing of the main elements are reminiscent of the work of Jacob Maris. Although the design

owes something to the example of the Barbizon school, it is the influence of Jules
Bastien-Lepage that is most marked. Even the thin square capitals of Crawhall's
signature in *Landscape with Cattle* are inspired by the example of Bastien-Lepage.
The large, carefully placed and blocky brushstrokes show his awareness of, and
probable use of, Bastien-Lepage's square-ended brushes, and both works show
Crawhall, like the French master, searching for consistency of light. The concern
with surface pattern, the use of overlapping forms and a restrained palette were
influences that were to continue long after Crawhall had turned from oil to
watercolour. Having stressed the foreign influences at work on Crawhall in this
period, it is equally important to acknowledge the influence on his art of the other
Glasgow Boys, in particular of Guthrie and Walton. Crawhall's carefully realised
integration of animal and landscape, the lighter tones and broader handling, were
achieved by working with Guthrie and Walton in the open air directly from
nature.

The Glasgow Boys championed the art of James Abbot McNeill Whistler and
were influenced by him. In his autobiography John Lavery wrote that 'Although
we at Glasgow worked with a richer palette than Whistler, we recognised in him
the greatest artist of the day and thought of his "Ten O'Clock Lecture" as the
Gospel of Art. Yet none of us ever saw him at work or knew his procedure.'[18] They
shared the American artist's belief that design was the surface organisation of
shapes within a picture space and that consequently, before being anything else, a
painting was a pattern of colour and form. Crawhall and Whistler met at the turn
of the century through their involvement in the International Society. They are
known to have respected each other's work and the lowering of tone in Crawhall's
later works on linen might well have been the result of Whistler's influence.

Contemporary reviewers continually remark on how similar Crawhall's work is
to the art of the Japanese print. One critic covering the International Society
exhibition of 1898 wrote that Crawhall's 'study of a *Black Cock* [pl 69] is a thing
that is without rival in the province of bird painting in England. His debt to the
Japanese is, of course, obvious; but here is no bastard imitation. It is a legitimate
influence put to splendid use.'[19] Although it is usually assumed that Crawhall
would have been made aware of Japanese prints through those owned by Walton
and Guthrie, it is entirely possible that his knowledge was, once again, due to his
father. An illustration in his father's book *Newcassel Sangs* and various drawings
in his scrapbooks show that Crawhall senior was aware of, if not a collector of,
Japanese prints. This interest is recorded in the Keene correspondence, when in
1878 Keene writes, 'Don't send back the Jap. [*sic*] books unless they are actually in
the way, as I am not wanting them, and I please myself with the idea that you may
appreciate them. The only reason why I should like to go to Paris, is to see the Jap.
collection, but I don't think I shall go.'[20] Crawhall's friend, John Lavery,
maintained that although '. . . the critics pointed out that he [Crawhall] must have
been strongly influenced by Japan, . . . he never saw a Japanese print until he was

twenty. He stood before it for a long time in silence, and then with great enthusiasm wished to buy it.'[21]

If Crawhall was interested in the art of Japan, it was an interest he could easily pursue in Glasgow which had strong trading links with the East. In 1877, the designer and teacher Christopher Dresser visited Japan as a British government observer and adviser. As a result of this visit the Japanese government in 1878 presented ceramics and samples of textiles and paper to the Corporation of Glasgow's art collection. Dresser, who was originally from Glasgow, returned in 1882 to deliver a lecture on Japan that coincided with the publication of his *Japan, Its Architecture, Art and Art Manufacture*. During this period a loan collection of Japanese and Persian art was displayed in the city's gallery. Although there is an evident kinship between Crawhall's art and the Japanese print, his work is more properly related to Chinese wash drawings on silk. If Crawhall visited the exhibition of oriental paintings at the British Museum in 1889 and at Dowdeswell's galleries in Bond Street, it could have inspired him to experiment with watercolour and gouache on holland linen. Many fundamental aspects of Crawhall's art reflect the values of oriental art: a brilliant and sensitive perception of colour, including the use of black as a colour; flattening forms by stark colour contrasts; stressing simplicity and refinement of form and line; daring to isolate a motif against an empty background; selecting fragmented images and unusual viewpoints; challenging traditional perspective and experimenting with distance and proportion. Unlike oriental artists Crawhall was interested in the accurate description of animal anatomy. He did, however, share their enduring love of nature and their ability to study, observe and record from memory the vital principles of motion and life as seen in natural forms.

Given the lack of documentary evidence it can only be a matter of opinion as to whether Crawhall arrived at these artistic values through oriental art or quite independently of it. His obituarist had no such doubts: 'I am convinced that with him it was an inner necessity so to eliminate, so to chasten and essentialise in the secret places of mind and heart, of spirit, too, his visual impressions.' He believed that Crawhall found, in the art of the Orient, 'a lofty and penetrating expressiveness such as alone would satisfy his own needs. In a word he did not copy the letter, but strove to aspire or attain the revealing spirit of oriental art. Long before Crawhall had seen a Japanese print or picture he did drawings which in marvellous degree unite objective and subjective realities – interpretative drawings that in negligible measure only depend for their appeal on factual accuracy, or mere verisimilitude.'[22]

One of the most important formative periods in the work of the Glasgow Boys was the years spent at Cockburnspath from 1883 to 1885. Cockburnspath, near Dunbar on the east coast of Scotland, was then on the post-road from Edinburgh to Glasgow. Windswept and austere, it had red-tiled and blue-slated cottages around an oblong square with an old market cross at the lower end. It was here

24
Annan
E. A. Walton, Joseph
Crawhall, George Walton,
James Guthrie,
James Whitelaw Hamilton
1884
Photograph
Private Collection

that 'for a few summers in the early 80s nearly every cottage had an artist lodger and easels were to be seen pitched in the gardens or in the square, in the fields close by, or near the little harbour in the rocks below the cluster of white cottages at the Cove.'[23] Here the Boys aimed to acquire a greater technical skill and a more developed sense of design, and to increase their study of values and lighting. As before, companionship was all important (pl 24). In 1883 Guthrie and Walton stayed at a Mrs Robertson's cottage near the Inn and Crawhall soon joined them. Other visitors were James Whitelaw Hamilton, George Henry, Thomas Corsan Morton and Arthur Melville. During one of these visits, probably in 1884, Crawhall writes to his mother, 'In a letter from Bloss she says you are going to Oban and as James has just come from those parts he has kindly written out a list of all that is to be seen, as where to stay etc., which I think you will find useful. I told Smith to send my picture back to Eldon Square as I want it for Glasgow at the end of the year and also . . . I am painting some big cows at the edge of a wood at present. [He then sketches the picture – now lost.] I think it will be a better picture than last year as far as it has gone, in fact I must make it so if I can. As to the dispute Bloss talks about James has brown hair and eyes and is thick set. Love to all, your loving son, Jos.'[24] Quite apart from confirming the closeness of their artistic community, this letter is interesting evidence that Crawhall worked on more oils than have survived and the sketch shows that these were in the style of other Glasgow Boy pictures.

In 1884 Guthrie took the factor's house at Dunglass by Cockburnspath, and rented a red-roofed barn in the village which he converted into a studio. While Guthrie continued to work in oil, Walton and Crawhall were increasingly turning

25
The Duckpond
c.1883–4
Watercolour on paper,
39.5×30.5
Private Collection

26
Pigs at the Trough
1884
Watercolour on paper,
26.0×46.0
Sir Norman and Lady
Macfarlane

to the medium of watercolour to record the inhabitants and landscape of the Berwickshire coast. There are striking similarities between Crawhall's *The Duck-pond* (pl 25) and Walton's *A Girl Feeding Ducklings* (sold at Sotheby's, 1987), both works presumably executed at Cockburnspath *c*.1883–4. *The Duckpond* reveals interesting details of Crawhall's early watercolour technique. There is extensive coverage of the paper and, never a purist, he has sparingly applied bodycolour throughout. The areas of light in the foreground and the whiteness of the ducks have been achieved by Crawhall scratching the paper when wet, thereby removing the upper layers. Unlike their early experiments in oil, there is 'no fumbling and no reaching after something not fully realised,' in the watercolours of Walton and Crawhall.[25] Both would go on to experiment with various materials on which to paint, including tinted paper, fine linen and silk.

With the exception of 'Grecian Williams' and William Leighton Leitch, water-colour in Scotland prior to 1870 had been practised primarily as an auxiliary to oils: watercolour sketches rather than drawings serving as studies for a finished work in oil. This changed in 1870 when artists like Sam Bough and William McTaggart began to use watercolour as an end in itself. The Scottish Society of Painters in Watercolours was founded in 1878 and, influenced by the water-colours of Israels, the Maris brothers, Bosboom and Mauve, young Scottish artists increasingly experimented with the medium. As late as 1918 one artist was

27
The Greyhound
c.1884
Watercolour on paper,
38.6×38.3
The Burrell Collection

28
Foxhounds – Jingling
1886
Watercolour heighter
bodycolour on paper,
51.8×34.3
The Burrell Collectio

29
The Byre
1887
Watercolour on paper,
34.5×32.7
Glasgow Art Gallery and
Museum

complaining that 'the day seems still far off when a more united appreciation will be based on a picture as a work of art, regardless of the value placed upon the medium in which it is produced.'[26] Crawhall's increasing use of watercolour makes one question how he himself regarded his professional status — did he consider himself as a gifted amateur or as a professional artist?

Necessarily executed on a smaller scale, watercolours were less visible in exhibitions and commanded much lower prices. This situation was slowly to change with the establishment of watercolour societies but during this period watercolours were still usually consigned to the minor rooms of an exhibition. Crawhall's choice, though, was not dictated by the need to sell — like Melville he was assured a purchaser almost as soon as a work was finished. The spontaneity and resulting freshness that the medium offered him were suitable for his summary and delicate vision of the world. In addition, more mundane considerations had their appeal — the materials were portable and it was no longer necessary to work in a studio.

Pigs at the Trough, 1884 (pl 26), *The Greyhound*, c.1884 (pl 27), *Foxhounds – Jingling Gate*, 1886 (pl 28), and *The Byre*, 1887 (pl 29), give some idea of Crawhall's development. Crawhall soon allows the support — that is the paper, canvas or linen — he was working on to do more of the work by supplying a background colour, allowing the artist merely to suggest form rather than describe it. Hartrick, in his autobiography, has left a valuable record of Crawhall's technique. 'When working in pure water-colour . . . he had a habit of putting the drawing under the tap with the water running, watching it till it came to the state he sought for; then, laying it flat, he would finish it with a few bold touches of sharp drawing or strong colour which brought out the character and life to perfection.'[27] Subsequent sponging and retouching, though, could entail the loss of the delicate surface bloom as in *The Greyhound*.

As soon as he had mastered the art of watercolour, Crawhall began to experiment with pastel. There was a strong revival of interest in pastel in the late nineteenth century. Artists like Whistler, Fantin-Latour, Degas, Sickert and Wilson Steer chose to work in this medium which was, essentially, drawing with colour. Works by these artists could be seen in Glasgow at loan exhibitions and in the galleries of dealers like Alexander Reid. In 1889 pastels by Scottish artists were on show at the Royal Scottish Academy. In the same year the Glasgow Institute of the Fine Arts held an exhibition exclusively for works in pastel, black and white and watercolour. A critic writing in the *Scottish Art Review* that year commented: 'Pastel, our newest craze, which has been eagerly seized by amateur and artist as a means of demonstrating "how to do", as opposed to "what to do", is the most recent tribute to the goddess of "technique".'[28]

Alexander Reid is said to have encouraged Guthrie to work in pastel and when the short-lived Society of Pastellists was founded in 1890, Guthrie was invited to join. He might have already worked in pastel at Cockburnspath.[29] His two most

30
The Goat
1889
Pastel on paper, 34.3×37.8
The Burrell Collection

important series of pastels, mainly of sea and landscapes with figures, date from a stay at Cambuskenneth in 1888, and at Helensburgh in 1890. Guthrie, in turn, persuaded his friends to try pastel. Walton, in 1888, had taken a studio at Cambuskenneth, near Stirling. In the autumn of 1888 he was joined there by Guthrie and Crawhall. Influenced by Guthrie's example, Crawhall worked on *The Goat* (pl 30) and *Hen and Chickens* (pl 31), and was sufficiently pleased with the latter to include it in the 1889 exhibition. Although Guthrie influenced Crawhall's handling of pastel, he was himself inspired by Crawhall's vision and his pastels

31
Hen and Chickens
1889
Pastel on paper, 62.5×48.8
The Burrell Collection

32
The Forge
1887
Watercolour on paper,
63.5×55.5
Sir Norman and Lady Macfarlane

33
Edward Arthur Walton
Joseph Crawhall
1884
Oil on canvas, 49.9×36.8
Scottish National Portrait
Gallery, Edinburgh

34
Black Spanish Cock
c.1893–1901
Gouache on linen,
19.0×12.6
The Burrell Collection

35
The Farmer's Boy
c.1894–9
Gouache on linen,
31.0×21.3
The Burrell Collection

The Ropewalk, 1888, and *The Smithy*, 1890, were inspired by Crawhall's watercolour *The Forge* (pl 32).

The work of the Glasgow Boys was not immediately appreciated by exhibition juries and the picture-buying public. Throughout the 1880s their works were often rejected, badly hung or criticised as unfinished, careless, too French, or 'impressionist'. In 1893 George Reid, President of the Royal Scottish Academy, complained that the 'so called impressionists have, unfortunately, some followers in Scotland. There is quite a school of them in Glasgow. . . . But what is this impressionism except, among the younger artists, the offerings of admiring incapacity in the shape of more or less dexterous imitation of some of the better known leaders of the movement in France? I greatly dislike young artists going in for this kind of thing. It is simply an impertinence. . . .'[30] The irony of such a comment was that, as the Boys specialised in depicting duckponds, cabbage patches and village scenes, their work was actually intensely local, yet was accused

of being foreign. By 1893, despite the criticism of the academic hierarchy, the
Glasgow Boys and Crawhall were receiving international acclaim.

In 1890 George Clausen persuaded Coutts-Lindsay of the Grosvenor Gallery in
London to have a Glasgow Boy room. Although most of the Boys had exhibited
extensively throughout Britain, this was the first time they had exhibited as a
group outside Scotland. The critical reception, though mixed, brought the Boys
renown and Adolphe Paulus immediately organised a showing of the Boys' work
in Munich. In Munich, Crawhall's *The Aviary* (pl 106) was awarded a gold medal
of the second class. Crawhall's father, in typically jovial form, writes, 'We received
Joe's gold (Munich) medal this morning – neat – worth possibly 3 or £4.'[31] In the
following months and years works by Crawhall and the Boys were to be seen in
Dresden, Berlin, Vienna, Budapest, Venice, St Petersburg, Bruges, Brussels, St
Louis, Chicago, Cincinnati, Philadelphia and New York. Their work was admired
and sold well, though Crawhall's watercolours, which were on loan from British
private collectors and unlike the other works in the exhibitions were not for sale,
must have frustrated prospective purchasers. A reviewer in the *St. Louis Life* in
1895 declared that one 'of the most remarkable men of the school is Joseph
Crawhall, Jr. Mr Crawhall paints birds and animals, generally in watercolour in a
manner that justly has been described as epigrammatic. *The Aviary*, the *Rabbit*
and the *Master of Hounds* are pictures which no other living artist could have
painted.'[32]

Few scholars have doubted the justice of including Joseph Crawhall in books
and exhibitions on Scottish painting and watercolour and in specific studies of the
Glasgow Boys.[33] The inscription on Walton's portrait of *Joseph Crawhall* (pl 33)
might seem to imply some aesthetic distinction; 'Joe Crawhall The Impressionist
by E. A. Walton The Realist'. However, Crawhall in choice of subject matter, in
style and technique and even in the exhibiting bodies he chose to become a
member of, quite clearly considered himself as one of the Boys. In later years when
Walton and Guthrie moved to London and later still when he himself moved to
Yorkshire, they continued to keep in touch. The major difference was that whilst
he, in works such as *Black Spanish Cock* (pl 34) and *The Farmer's Boy* (pl 35), was
freer to continue to work on the themes, and develop along the lines of their shared
aims, the others, with wives and families to support, turned to portraiture for a
secure income. Crawhall had been influenced by, and in turn influenced, the work
of the Boys and John Lavery might not have been exaggerating when he claimed
that Crawhall was 'the artist to whom the Glasgow School owed its greatest
distinction.'[34]

CHAPTER
3
TANGIER AND SPAIN

Recently described as a 'fading old queen of a city', Tangier's decaying hotel façades, Edwardian villas and eccentric community of expatriates remind us of its former status during the first five decades of this century as one of the most stylish resorts of the Mediterranean. Then, as now, the city was home to a lively community of writers, artists and diplomats attracted to a city which, though perched close to the southernmost tip of Europe, was quite unlike any European city. One traveller, writing at the end of the last century, went so far as to say that despite being 'almost within a stone's throw of Europe . . . the unlucky tourist might fancy that some demon had taken him by the neck while asleep and dropped him on another planet . . .'[1]

Throughout the nineteenth century, Tangier, with its walled Medina of white houses and painted minarets, intersected by narrow streets and dominated by the Kasbah, was perceived by the writers, artists and the few tourists who dared travel there as a mystical, magical place. Its bright light, brilliant colour and distinctive lifestyle attracted many generations of European artists. In the nineteenth century, French masters such as Berain, Huet, Géricault, Decamps, Fromentin and Regnault visited Tangier. It inspired the large, frieze-like panoramas of laden camels crossing the desert, or exotic fantasies, usually highly coloured, which were the staple of the artists of the Romantic school.

One of the greatest masters of French art, Eugène Delacroix (1798–1863), was to make something quite different of his short stay in 1832. Revitalised by what he felt was a rediscovery of the classical dignity and beauty of the Homeric age, Delacroix filled his sketchbooks with observations of African life and authentic details of costume. These watercolours, like the *Journal* he kept, provided him with a rich store of pictorial motifs for paintings executed many years later: *The Fanatics of Tangier* (Jerome Hill, New York), *The Sultan of Morocco and his Entourage* (Musée des Augustins, Toulouse), a series of five oils on the theme of the *Fantasia arabe*, and for *The Jewish Wedding in Morocco* (Louvre). In his *Journal* Delacroix records how the people of Tangier 'live exactly as they did in ancient times. An outdoor life and carefully closed houses, the women withdrawn from the world . . . The chief men of the town squat in the sun at street-corners to talk, or perch like a row of birds in the shop of some merchant . . . Everything is ruled by custom and tradition . . . It must be hard for them to understand the easy-going ways of Christians and the restlessness that sends us perpetually seeking after new ideas. We notice a thousand things in which they are lacking, but their ignorance is the foundation of their peace and happiness . . . In many ways they are closer to nature than we – their clothes, for instance and the shape of their shoes. Hence there is beauty in everything they do. But we, with our corsets, narrow shoes, and tubular clothing, are lamentable objects. We have gained science at the cost of grace.'[2]

Many of Joseph Crawhall's British contemporaries, artists like Robert Bevan and William Rothenstein, visited Tangier at the end of the nineteenth century. Scottish artists also travelled there, some for a few weeks, others remaining for the rest of their lives. Glasgow Boy visitors included T. Millie Dow, Arthur Melville, John Lavery, Alexander Mann and William Kennedy.[3] Mann and Lavery perfected sketch-like techniques in their panoramic views of the city and its surrounding countryside and depicted the life of the city's inhabitants, a people who still believed in the 'evil eye'. Unlike most artist visitors to Tangier Crawhall was not interested in portraying the social or physical context, concentrating instead on capturing and conveying the characteristics of Tangier's domestic animals, whether on the hills surrounding the city or in the market-place.

Crawhall's experience in Paris in 1882 and summers spent working with Guthrie and Walton at Brig o' Turk, Crowland, Cockburnspath and Cambuskenneth had eventually convinced him that watercolour rather than oil was the medium most suited to his perception of the world, to his method of working and to his itinerant lifestyle. It was during visits to Tangier, in particular those of 1887 and 1888, that he was to perfect his watercolour technique. *Donkey, Tangier* (pl 36), 1887, shows how far Crawhall had progressed from the dark tones and thickly applied strokes of oils like *A Lincolnshire Stream* (pl 20). The composition, with its high horizon line and consequent flattening of the picture plane, is reminiscent of works by Walton and Henry. A broad thin wash of blue indicates

36
Donkey, Tangier
1887
Watercolour heightened with
bodycolour on paper,
39.0×43.0
Paul Mellon Collection,
Upperville, Virginia

the sky, but already Crawhall is allowing the material he is working on to do much of the work, for the sandy foreground is suggested by the paper itself. Short stabs of green indicate the scrubby grasses on the horizon line, while looser and random strokes of brown and blue convey the aridity of the land. Crawhall has concentrated his attention on depicting the profiled donkey and the herd-boy lying, for protection from the sun's heat, in its shadow. Both boy and donkey are described in strokes of warm brown, a brown relieved by touches of blue and by the hasty indication of the coloured trappings of the donkey. A deeper blue, the shadow cast by the animal on the ground, although realistic, serves simultaneously to heighten

37
Anonymous
Joseph Crawhall Seated,
North Africa
c.1884–93
Photograph
Scottish National Portrait
Gallery, Edinburgh

the feeling of heat and provide a focal point for the composition. Also typical is the careful placing, the harmonious colouring and the calligraphic style of Crawhall's signature – more often than not it plays an important role in the overall design. Without resorting to the use of white or grey, Crawhall successfully conveys a bleached lightness and the sensation of a searing heat.

It is not known when Joseph Crawhall first visited Tangier, although it has been suggested that he went there directly after his stay in Paris in 1882.[4] However, it is most likely that his first visit was in 1884 and he continued to go there until 1893. The most thorough documentation survives for his visits of 1887 and 1888 in family letters and, unusually for Crawhall, by dated works. Like most travellers he visited Tangier in winter, sometimes staying for as long as six months. As one friend remarked, no 'place could have suited him better than the Tangier of those days. In it he found exactly all he wanted for his art.'[5]

How would Crawhall have heard about Tangier and why should he have chosen to travel there? In a letter to Crawhall's father in 1880 Keene writes, 'I met Robert S. Watson, who came for a day to Foster's. His yarns about his travels in Morocco were amusing, and I'm curious to hear the full particulars in the book he is writing.'[6] Three years later Keene writes that 'Birket Foster has gone to Spain, Tangier etc., for six weeks.'[7] In this same letter 'young Joe' is mentioned as exhibiting at the Royal Academy. Consequently, at home, or in any of the artistic circles he frequented, Crawhall would have heard of Tangier's appeal as a sketching ground.

Crawhall was possibly attracted by the eccentric lifestyle of the city, a lifestyle captured by his friend Robert Bontine Cunninghame Graham in a series of essays, *Writ in Sand*. 'Those were the days when Tangier was one of the most fascinating places in the whole world to live in; a miniature Constantinople, it had representatives of every Court in Europe, a consul-general from the United States, and ministers or consuls, who behaved like ministers, from many South American Republics. Flags of the various nations fluttered from half a hundred houses in the town. Adventurers who styled themselves presidents of Patagonia, kings of Araucania, and other hypothetic states, hoisted the flags of their fantastic countries, and whilst their money lasted, if they were presentable, spoke "diplomatic French", were not seen drunk in public, or committed any flagrant misdemeanour, were received as cordially in the tolerant society of the place as if they had been representatives of real countries to be found upon the map. The Moors looked on them all with awe, mixed with amusement . . . Tangier was then one of the dirtiest towns in the whole world, outside of China, but perfectly safe to live in, for robberies were rare and crimes of violence practically unknown. . . .'[8]

Crawhall may equally have been drawn to the city for his health. Tangier has an exceptionally temperate, dry and sunny climate, ideal for someone like Crawhall who suffered throughout his life from lung problems. Nevertheless, from his father's letters it is clear that Crawhall was not free from health problems, even in Tangier. In 1888 he writes, 'More trouble – Joe's been quite laid up in Tangier with dysentery – he's not too strong I fancy he hasn't a constitution to play with these varied climates – however, he's doing good work.'[9] The following year he writes to his sister Mary that 'Joe writes occasionally from Tangier but I fear his health is not so satisfactory as we'd like – I almost fear he cannot stand the climate. . . .' and on 17 April, 'Joe writes in better health though far from strong. . . .'[10]

Another reason why Tangier was attractive to artists was the low cost of living. In a letter to his wife, Alexander Mann describes how 'Yesterday I saw Lavery and Kennedy and they both think of going to Tangier in the spring. They say that Crawhall lives at Tangier at the rate of 6/- a day and for that he has two horses, a

38
Sheep in a Meadow
1887
Watercolour heightened with
bodycolour on paper,
21.3×27.8
Private Collection

39
Goats on a Hillside – Tangier
1887
Watercolour heightened with
bodycolour, 40.4×34.6
The Burrell Collection

man servant and a maidservant besides his board and lodging . . .'[11] Despite outward appearances and statements to the contrary, Crawhall did take financial matters into consideration.

Tangier was relatively easy to travel to. One took the P&O line from London to Gibraltar, and then made the short crossing from Gibraltar to Tangier. There being no port or pier, passengers were carried ashore on the backs of wading natives, though by the 1890s rowing boats were used. Once on land, clamouring porters and guides would vie for attention, eventually steering the visitor to an hotel. In the 1890s Crawhall is known to have stayed at both the Calpe Hotel and the New York Hotel, the latter situated outside the town on the beach. Earlier, in the late 1880s, he stayed at the Hotel Continental which still overlooks Tangier Bay. Reached via the Medina it was 'a very clean, comfortable, and almost elegant abode; and on the beach side it has a number of much-coveted rooms with a fine view of the ocean, and the coast and harbour scenery. Below the balcony is a wilderness of cactus. . . .'[12] The photograph of Crawhall, palette in hand, cigarette in mouth and with a gentle smile playing on his lips, might well have been taken near the hotel (pl 37).

40
The Goatherd
1888
Watercolour on paper,
25.8×22.7
The Burrell Collection

From the Hotel Continental it was only a few paces into the city itself. Then, as now, the visitor was advised to take a local guide. Writing in 1897, one traveller describes the 'labyrinth of narrow, tortuous lanes, or rather passageways, flanked by small, square, white houses, devoid of windows . . . whose outward appearance suggests a cross between a prison and a convent. In many of the streets nothing can be seen but the white of the buildings and the blue of the sky; . . . Almost all the streets are littered with decayed vegetables, feathers, rags, bones, and sometimes the bodies of dead animals poison the air.'[13] Clad in jellabah and fez, the inhabitants gave the city 'the look of a vast monastery of Dominican monks. . . . Of this shrouded population the one half moves about slowly, noiselessly, sedately, almost as though trying to escape observation, and the other remains either seated or stretched at full-length along the walls, before the shops, or in the angles of the buildings, immovable, with fixed gaze, like the petrified characters in their own legends.'[14]

Crawhall's earliest dated Tangier watercolours however, those of 1887, are of scenes outside the town itself. *Sheep in a Meadow* (pl 38), *Donkey* (pl 36), *Goats on a Hillside* (pl 39) and *The Goatherd* of 1888 (pl 40) show how consistently Crawhall responded to the landscape both in terms of composition and of technique. Thin and transparent wet washes are juxtaposed with opaque notations, pale blue strokes of bodycolour simultaneously suggesting the strength of the light and defining the form and volume of the animal or figure depicted.

It was during his trip of 1887 that Crawhall was accompanied by the Edinburgh animal artist Robert Alexander (1840–1923) and his son Edwin (1870–1926).

41
The Goat
c.1893–1900
Gouache on linen,
43.5×46.5
National Gallery of Scotland,
Edinburgh

42
Arab Ploughing with
Bullocks, Tangier
1889
Pastel on paper, 28.3×45.1
National Gallery of Scotland,
Edinburgh

Edwin Alexander specialised in flora and fauna and although he was to be much influenced by Crawhall, his work was essentially imitative and he lacked Crawhall's ability to suggest movement. Edwin Alexander later adopted Crawhall's use of the difficult medium of gouache on linen. No evidence has been found of Crawhall having worked on linen before the early 1890s, and although *The Goat* (pl 41) might, from the evidence of the colours and the landscape, have been executed in Tangier, it must date from his last visit there in 1893.

As we have seen in Chapter 2, Crawhall experimented with pastel in 1889 under the influence of Guthrie, and a remarkable demonstration of his ability in handling this medium is seen in *Arab Ploughing with Bullocks, Tangier*, 1889 (pl 42). The pastel is applied in blocks of colour akin to the application of the oil in *A Lincolnshire Pasture* (pl 22), and consequently is more structured and deliberate in appearance than the watercolours of the same period. It was done on the outskirts of Tangier, although one traveller records that he saw little in the way of agriculture near Tangier: on 'one single occasion I recollect seeing someone engaged in cultivating the earth; an Arab was driving a donkey and a goat hitched to the tiny plough of curious design, probably the shape of those in use 4,000 years ago; he was making a furrow so small as scarcely to be visible, in a field covered with stones and weeds. . . . I was assured that it was not uncommon to see a woman and a donkey hitched together to the plough. . . .'[15]

When staying at the Hotel Continental, Crawhall would not have had far to walk to the Petit Socco – a market-place – and then up the long narrow street leading to the Grand Socco (pl 43). The Grand Socco was the centre of the town and it was here, late in 1887 and in 1888, that Crawhall was to find suitable subjects for a magnificent series of watercolours. In his autobiography John Lavery evocatively describes the Socco in the morning when it 'is in full blast packed with a mass of shouting men and screaming women, mingled with the silvery tinkle of the bell of the water-carrier and the many notes coming from donkey noise, horse noise, camel noise, sheep noise, and goat noise. Add to this the uplifted voices of the halt, the maimed, and the blind pleading for alms from the Christian who, as a rule, is mounted and indifferent to everything but his own importance as he forces those on foot to make way. But in the afternoon the place is empty except for the snake-charmer and his audience, and the story-teller and those who squat in a circle and listen with deep interest to his tales of love and adventure.'[16]

Crawhall's *The Snake Charmer* (pls 44, 45) evokes the mystery of the charmer's performance without hinting at the violence that some writers record. One traveller, writing in 1891, recalls seeing one particular charmer with five snakes accompanied by a band that consisted of two stringless snare drums and something that was a cross between a bagpipe and an oboe. As the snakes were venomous the charmer was reputed to swallow a plant leaf as an antibody, but the visitor recorded with some horror that the charmer allowed the snakes to bite each other and the small boy accompanying him, and then expected to be paid for his cruelty.[17] Crawhall isolates the white-robed snake charmer whom he had observed against a white wall. Seated under delicately painted flowering branches, which partially shade him, he concentrates on the large drum he is playing and seemingly not on the snakes, a tangled web of curving line and colour in the right foreground. The compositional diagonal has been carefully considered and the

43
Anonymous
Market Day, Grand Socco,
Tangier
c.1900
Postcard

45
Anonymous
Snake Charmer, Tangier
c.1900
Postcard

whole is a muted harmony of blues, mauves, creams and greens.

The Snake Charmer might well demonstrate the influence on Crawhall of the watercolours of Arthur Melville (1855–1904) for it is unusual to find Crawhall taking such care to record accurately the features of a human figure. There are many similarities in style and technique between the two artists, but it is difficult to know whether it was Melville who influenced Crawhall's watercolour technique or vice versa, or whether both arrived at similar results quite independently. D. S. MacColl made the unusual comment that Melville 'leaned to pictorial formula rather than to naturalism, a formula learned from Mr Crawhall. It was brilliantly applied in some of his watercolours. . . .'[18] Melville's biographer writes that Crawhall 'was nearer to Melville than any other painter of their generation. Of the two he was the more subtle draughtsman.'[19] Later she adds 'The Glasgow School owed much to him, he owed little or nothing to any of them. His kindred spirit was Joseph Crawhall . . . but Crawhall was nearer to Degas than was Melville to any one of the French Impressionists.'[20]

In the 1880s Melville and Crawhall had worked together at Cockburnspath (1883–4) and at Cambuskenneth (1887) and would certainly have shared ideas. During these visits Crawhall might well have seen Melville's *The Snake Charmer* (Private Collection) painted in 1883 in Edinburgh, from a sketch done in Baghdad in 1882. Both Melville's and Crawhall's watercolours of this subject were included in the Royal Scottish Society of Painters in Watercolours exhibition of 1888, where Melville was one of those responsible for the hanging. Based on the east coast of Scotland, Melville was largely independent of the Glasgow Boys but was friendly with Walton and Guthrie. Like so many of the Boys, Melville preferred to practise art rather than to theorise about it. He had a good-natured disposition and one writer records how the 'visits of Melville to his western friends

44
The Snake Charmer
1888
Watercolour on paper,
62.5×52.5
Private Collection

were always occasions of stimulus and propaganda. There was something tonic in his speech; his big, handsome courageous presence infested all the group with joie de vivre and the self assurance it badly needed though its brave words might suggest otherwise.' The same writer concludes '. . . Three men who were not Glasgow at all have, curiously, had the most wonderful influence on the Glasgow School – MacTaggart, Crawhall and Melville – Melville perhaps most of all.'[21]

It seems likely that Melville chose to specialise in watercolour long before Crawhall had made a similar decision. Certainly it was his favoured medium for recording the scenes during his travels in Cairo and beyond in 1880–2. Melville, however, worked directly from nature, his original watercolour sketches serving him as models for finished watercolours executed in the studio, sometimes years later. Like Crawhall, Melville had a tremendous pictorial sense and could capture dazzling light, transparent shadows and the sensation of crowds in movement. Melville's technique is certainly close to that used by Crawhall for the watercolours he executed in Tangier in 1887 and 1888. Melville would first impregnate the paper with Chinese white, saturate it, and rinse it. He would then make a drawing indicating the essential lines of the composition before applying the colour with vigorous brush strokes, finally sponging out any superfluous detail. Next he would run in more reds or blues, with the stronger colours being added when the paper was nearly dry.[22] Crawhall's method was similar, the only difference being that he rarely indicated broad lines of composition with pencil drawing: he worked on the paper in colour directly. Melville, who unlike Crawhall had to earn a living by his art, often produced as many as eight sketches in one week.

The 'blottesque' or stainy appearance of Melville's watercolours did not always meet with critical approval. Melville's *Call to Prayer, Midan Mosque, Baghdad*, when exhibited at the Dudley Gallery in 1883, received mixed critical reviews, one writer stating '. . . we must decline to believe that the representative art of painting fulfills its purpose when it is shown in dabs, blurs and splashes of paint as in the drawing we are referring to.'[23] James Caw, writing in 1908 of Melville's late watercolours, could just as easily have been describing those by Crawhall: '. . . beauty of colour often laid in broad simple masses sharply juxtaposed, and always retaining the glow and sparkle obtainable from the paper, which in many passages is little more than delicately stained, and a more matured and masterly sense of disposition, which, working on a more imposing scale than formerly, made more of the great plain surfaces and used accent more sparingly but with greatly enhanced cunning.' He continues: 'An impressionist in the more restricted sense, keenly and sensitively appreciative of light, colour and movement, living in the external show of things, and expressing himself with vitality and assured mastery, Arthur Melville brought the scintillating splendour and many-coloured movement of the south before one with the vividness of dreams or the intensity

46
A Moorish Packhorse
1888
Watercolour on paper,
42.5×33.5
Glasgow Art Gallery and
Museum

48
Picketed Horses, Tangier
1888
Watercolour on paper,
32.7×51.2
The Burrell Collection

and freshness of impressions one might have received at first hand in moments of exceptional receptivity.'[24]

Health, ease of travel and a comparatively cheap cost of living have been offered as reasons for Crawhall's trips to Tangier. However, another important attraction for Crawhall would have been the availability of and universal use of the horse. Crawhall loved horses, and the cheapness of horses in Tangier would have been an important factor in his decision to travel there. One visitor recalled that these 'were the dear old uncivilised days of Tangier when there was literally not a single road nor vehicle in the whole country, and when, if you wanted to get from one place to another, you had to ride, or else go on your own flat feet. Even when you went out to dinner in Tangier you had to ride – ladies and all; and if it happened to be pouring with rain – well, so much the worse for your varnished shoes or the skirt of your frock; but nobody minded.'[25]

Resting horses provide the motif for three important watercolours executed in Tangier and inspired by scenes in the Grand Socco: *A Moorish Packhorse* (pl 46), *Barb Horse in Stable* (pl 47) and *Picketed Horses* (pl 48). There is a certain sadness of atmosphere in *A Moorish Packhorse* with the beast of burden tied to one of the stalls of the Grand Socco. Exhibited at the Royal Scottish Society of Painters in Watercolours in 1888, this work was available for sale for a mere £18.

An equally prevalent means of transport, of course, was the camel, and Crawhall's watercolour *Camels* (pl 49) was again the result of a frequent scene witnessed in the Grand Socco in Tangier, the distinctive double-gate in the

47
Barb Horse in Stable
1886
Watercolour heightened with
bodycolour, 46.4×36.3
The Burrell Collection

background confirming the Grand Socco as the location (pl 50). During the day flour, nuts, butter, dates, fruit and coloured candy were on sale in the Socco. Mules and camels would file across the large open space of the Socco, surrounded by booths and tents, and teeming with men and women, donkeys and oxen, and overflowing with wares for sale. Ten of Crawhall's Tangier scenes, including the *Camels*, were on view in the Central Exchange Art Gallery in Newcastle in 1888. A reviewer praised the 'remarkable display of colour. Unlike the uniform smooth, painting which is characteristic of British art, his pictures are patchy, and after the style of the modern impressionist school, about which there is considerable excitement and enthusiasm in London . . . The artists who have seen the pictures admit their eccentricity, and at the same time admit the display of artistic skill, and the marvellous appreciation of the colour and atmosphere which characterises the district of Tangier . . . Mr Crawhall has succeeded in giving a twofold impression of obscurity arising from excessive light on the one hand and marvellous arrangement of colours on the other . . . The picture containing the camels is in reality a study, because at first sight it is very difficult to recognise what the animals are, but, once catching the idea of the picture, they are easily recognised. It has been observed that visitors who have a taste for art more frequently inspect the pictures from the easel of Mr Crawhall than any other in the gallery.'[26]

The British Legation was the centre of a gay and informal social life in Tangier where activities included pig-sticking, racing, polo and hunt-meetings. Crawhall took an active part in these activities – indeed he seems to have been one of the leading lights. An invaluable record of Crawhall in Tangier is to be found in the writings of Robert Bontine Cunninghame Graham who had known Crawhall in Glasgow and was to keep in touch with him after Crawhall moved to Yorkshire. Cunninghame Graham, or Don Roberto as he was known, was one of the most picturesque figures of the day. Landowner, adventurer, writer, rancher and politician, he was eventually forced to sell his ancestral home at Gartmore and move to Ardoch, near Cardross, another family estate. Possessed of great wit and a caustic tongue, much of the theatricality of his character is caught in the full-length and life-size portrait of him by John Lavery (pl 51). A Whistlerian 'harmony in brown', Lavery has succeeded in capturing the essence of his sitter's unconventional personality. George Bernard Shaw used Cunninghame Graham as the model for his character Captain Brassbound and commented on this portrait: 'He is, I understand, a Spanish hidalgo, hence the superbity of his portrait by Lavery (Velazquez being no longer available). He is, I know, a Scottish laird. How he continues to be authentically the two things at the same time is no more intelligible to me than the fact that everything that has ever happened to him seems to have happened in Paraguay or Texas instead of Spain or Scotland.'[27]

In an essay entitled 'Creeps' in his collection *Writ in Sand*, Cunninghame Graham portrays the Crawhall of the Tangier period as a silent but witty, somewhat dissolute character. 'As he stood in the smoking room of the Hotel

49
Camels
1888
Watercolour on paper,
24.0×34.3
The Burrell Collection

50
Anonymous
Two Gates, Tangier
c.1900
Postcard

51
John Lavery
R. B. Cunninghame Graham
1893
Oil on canvas, 203.2×107.9
Glasgow Art Gallery and Museum

52
Anonymous
Joseph Crawhall (centre) and The Tangier Hounds
c.1890
Photograph

53
Doctor's Crop Acts like a Hot Seidletz Powder
c.1891
Pencil and watercolour, 12.1×19.3
Ewan Mundy Fine Art

54
Lady on Horseback Spearing Wild Boar
c.1902
Ink and wash on paper, 15.1×20.0
The Burrell Collection

55
Mary, Eileen and President
c.1902
Ink and wash on paper,
15.1×20.0
The Burrell Collection

Continental in Tangier, dressed in a faded red hunting-coat that had turned almost the colour of a mulberry through exposure to the weather and the fierce sun of Northern Africa, holding a velvet cap in one hand, and in the other his crop and a pair of weather-stained rein-worn dog-skin gloves, few would have taken him for a great artist and a man of genius. He had the air of a second whip to a provincial pack of hounds down on his luck and looking for a place. His cord riding breeches hardly met his cracked and ill-cleaned boots. His spurs were rusty, and had it not been for his hands, well-shaped and delicate, his sleek dark head, and deep brown, almost chocolate eyes, eyes that impelled you to follow them. . . .' He continues: 'Although he spoke to no one, it was evident that he had seen not only every person in the room, but every object in it. For a considerable time he sat, turning over listlessly the pages of *The Field*, and drinking several stiff whiskies and sodas, that had no effect upon him, except to seem to seal his lips more firmly, not that it seemed a voluntary act, but something born with him, as were his lustrous eyes or his sleek head. His slightly bandy legs he had acquired through early riding, for he was seldom off a horse, holding that Providence would have bestowed four legs on man had he intended him to go afoot.'[28]

What emerges so clearly here is Crawhall's love of the horse (pl 52). Tangier provided him with a wealth of opportunities not only for the depiction of his beloved horse, but also for riding. Another distinctive member of the horse-loving community in Tangier was Bernardino de Velasco, Duke of Frias (Hereditary

Grand Constable of Castile, Count of Oropesa, of Haro and a Grandee of Spain). Quick-witted and a good linguist, Frias eventually lost an extensive inheritance through gambling and died impoverished. Good-looking and charming, Frias, like Crawhall, was a perfect horseman. According to Cunninghame Graham, Frias 'entered into partnership with Crawhall . . . a kindred spirit and as fine a rider as himself, to hunt the Tangier hounds.' Frias was Master and Crawhall the first whip. 'Nothing was stranger than to see Frias . . . and Crawhall at a meet of the Tangier pack: Frias immaculately dressed in pink, his whip in a weather-stained mulberry-coloured hunting frock. . . . The pack was a collection such as it would be difficult to match in any country, with its three couple of mangy-looking foxhounds, from Gibraltar, with several mongrels of undecided race . . . and three or four half-bred fox-terriers. Foxes were scarce, and the heterogeneous pack ran wildly . . . the terriers snapping at the other dogs or fighting fiercely with one another. Anyone who had a horse came out.'[29]

On many occasions the second whip at these meets was George Denholm Armour (1864–1949), the sporting artist and illustrator. In his autobiography, *Bridle and Brush*, Denholm Armour, like Lavery and Cunninghame Graham, gives us precious details of Crawhall's life, for the two, both keen huntsmen, were to become lifelong friends. Born in Scotland, Denholm Armour studied at the Royal Scottish Academy life school in Edinburgh. His early work, in oil, *Sympathy* 1885, showing a terrier with bandaged leg watched by a small dog, was typically Victorian in both its subject and treatment. His illustrated books, usually of a sporting nature, demonstrate that, like May and Crawhall, he had an economical and expressive use of line and a keen sense of humour. However, he was to make his fortune from commissions for portraits of mounted riders and of hounds.

Denholm Armour visited Tangier for the first time in 1885 with Robert Alexander to paint and to find cheap horses and he stayed as long as his money held out. In his autobiography he elaborates on their hunting activities: 'There were no regular coverts, and we drew the open hillsides, which were covered with palmetto scrub, and found plenty of good red foxes . . . Earth-stopping in a country like that was almost impossible, and, in consequence, a mule carrying mining tools and a fox terrier, was a usual accompaniment to our party . . . Horses were cheap, all Barb stallions of about fifteen hands or less . . . Hard and sound. . . .'[30]

In 1936 Denholm Armour published an article, illustrated with sketches by Crawhall that had been saved by the author. *The Lighter Side of a Great Artist* describes their hunting activities in Tangier. Although the sketches capture humorous scenes, Crawhall does not seem to have worked these up into finished works of art. Denholm Armour explains that most 'of these sketches had a wash of colour, which made them decorative things, quite apart from their action and humour. Joe never valued them at all, and anyone, who chanced to be with him at the time, could have them.'[31] One such scene is *Doctor's Crop Acts like a Hot Seidletz Powder* (pl 53).

Another activity associated with the Hunt was the Tangier Hunt Cup. In *Bridle and Brush*, Denholm Armour records that Crawhall, 'a beautiful natural horseman . . . in Tangier was our champion jockey during the various times we were there together, and when any races were on the tapis, he was in great request.'[32] A family sketchbook in Newcastle Public Library contains the programme for the Tangier Hunt Steeple-Chase of Saturday, 19 April 1890. A glance at the names of Crawhall's fellow committee members is evidence of the nature of the society of which he was a part. The President was Sir William Kirby Green and the Stewards included the Italian, Belgian and German Ministers, the Consul-General for Sweden and the Rt. Hon. Sir John Drummond Hay. As Honorary Secretary, Crawhall had compiled the following rules:

1. Members of the Hunt only to ride.
2. Entries close Thursday April 17th at noon, to J. C. Ansaldo Esq. Continental Hotel.
3. The race to be ridden as far as possible, in proper Hunting costume.
4. Should there be any doubt regarding a horse being qualified to run according to the conditions of The Tangier Hunt Cup, a certificate from the M.F.H. should be obtained.

A cup value £25 added to a sweep'stakes of $5 for all horses and ponies which have been regularly hunted with the Tangier Hounds. Second horse to save his stake. Catch weights.

The actual race itself took place just outside Tangier, over four miles, from Mezenanah to Bubana. Crawhall's horse in 1890 was the Drone, and other horses running included Ugly, the Flea and Dan Dancer. It was Frias who won the first of these Hunt Challenge Cup events, but after successive wins in 1891, 1892 and 1893, Crawhall won the Cup on Dan Dancer, a horse that was a cross between a Barb stallion and a Spanish mare.[33] These meetings were followed by a Hunt dinner and Major-General Lord Edward Gleichen recalls watching Crawhall at one such dinner: 'I remember a quite magnificent sketch of a jumping horse he painted on the tablecloth . . . with the aid of a burnt match, some mustard, some red wine and the dregs of a bottle of Worcester Sauce.'[34]

Another activity that the community participated in was pig-sticking. According to Denholm Armour the ground for this was about seventeen miles outside Tangier around a country called 'Sharf-le-a-Kaab'. 'The largest boar I saw killed measured thirty-six inches to the shoulder.' He records that the 'best exponent of the spear' was Jack Green, the son of the British ambassador.[35] Many memoirs of the period mention this sport, recounting tales of heroism – as ever, except in

56
President (John Lavery) in Morocco
c.1902
Ink and watercolour on paper, 15.0×10.0
The Burrell Collection

57
Lady Riding a Camel
c.1902
Ink and wash on paper, 15.3×11.4
The Burrell Collection

sketches, Crawhall never recorded his personal experiences. Five of his sketches illustrate an article 'After Tangier Pig' written by Frias that appeared in the *Pall Mall Magazine* in 1901. Frias acknowledges Crawhall's assistance, saying 'I am indebted to the kindness of my old friend and fellow-hunter in Morocco . . . for the illustrations of a scene in which for many years he was one of the best over a rough country.'[36] In his article Frias explains the intricacies of the sport and the means of gaining permission to hunt and adds 'The meets are attended by Europeans of both sexes and there have been occasions on which ladies have taken a spear – aye, and killed their pig.' Just such an occasion is humorously imagined in a magnificent sketch contained in a letter from Crawhall to Mary Auras (pl 54). The letter also contains a sketch of *Mary, Eileen and President* riding towards Tangier (pl 55).

The President of the letter was another artist friend from the Glasgow days, John Lavery (1856–1941). On completion of his commemoration picture of the *State Visit of Queen Victoria to the Glasgow Exhibition* (Glasgow Art Gallery and

Museum) Lavery made his first visit to Tangier in 1890, no doubt encouraged by Crawhall. Lavery was fascinated by life in Tangier and he and Crawhall shared the company of men like Walter Harris, Bibi Carleton and Cunninghame Graham. Lavery bought a villa on the Old Mountain Road on the outskirts of Tangier just after the turn of the century and he was to return there regularly over the next fifteen years (pl 56).

Although of all the Glasgow Boys Lavery's work was to be the most consistently that of a 'painter of modern life', from the 1890s portraiture dominated his output. Born in Belfast, Lavery served his apprenticeship with an artist-

58
John Lavery
Spring
1904
Oil on canvas, 191.0 × 123.0
Musee d'Orsay, Paris

photographer in Glasgow before going to Paris and Grez to study and work. In France he was influenced by, and moved towards, decorative naturalism, synthesising the influence of Bastien-Lepage and Whistler. In his autobiography he relates how Bastien-Lepage advised him: 'Always carry a sketchbook. Select a person – watch him – then put down as much as you remember. Never look twice. At first you will remember very little, but continue and you will soon get complete action.'[37] The perfection of the visual memory was an accepted goal of French academic training and, given Crawhall's own training, it is not surprising that Lavery and Crawhall shared a mutual search for perceptual precision and economy.[38]

Tangier provided a necessary release for Lavery. Instead of commissioned

59
'How Crawhall Pictured a Friend in the Boer War'
c.1891
Watercolour on paper,
18.1×21.3
Private Collection

portraits, his work here consisted of oil sketches of street views, moonlight studies, snake charmers, the orange market, the Jewish quarter, the two Soccos, the Kasbah and the mosque. 'Lavery's colour underwent a gradual change after his first visit to Africa . . . a flattening of tone and a greater breadth and resilience in the effective harmony of his paint.'[39] These oils are not brightly coloured, but have the soft and silver greys of the true Orient and a marvellous sense of design. Three major exhibitions of Lavery's work included a hundred and fifty Tangier studies, at the Goupil Gallery in 1891 and 1908 and at the Leicester Gallery in 1904. Although Lavery and Crawhall were attracted by similar subjects in Tangier their technique and medium were essentially different. Lavery made studies from a model, or outside from life and would then work the sketches up in his studio. Lavery's *The Snake Charmers*, 1891 (Private Collection), is dark and static in comparison to the freshness and brilliance of Crawhall's treatment of the same subject.

Crawhall had been a witness at the marriage of Lavery and his first wife in 1889 and had a special affection for the daughter of this first marriage, Eileen. After the early death of her mother, Eileen regularly visited the Crawhall home at Brandsby in Yorkshire. In his autobiography, Lavery writes that although Crawhall 'never allowed anyone to watch him work . . . he made an exception in her case, and the two became inseparable friends. He made endless sketches for her on the pages of an old washing-book which fortunately she valued sufficiently to make into a scrapbook.'[40]

A third member of the Lavery household was Mary Auras. In his autobiography Lavery says he met Mary during one of the winters that he spent in Germany.[41] Mary was the niece of a well-known painter and he was introduced to her in the Unten den Linden by the German artist Auguste Neven du Mont.[42] Lavery brought the sixteen-year-old Mary with him from Germany to London, where she acted as a companion to his young daughter Eileen and worked as a model for him. The exact nature of their relationship is not clear. A card to Lavery from Mary, of 1903, implies by its subject matter and substance that there might have been a romantic attachment between the two. The cartoon of Romeo and Juliet drawn on the card suggests that Mary's English was improving. Mary writes, 'How you like my Romeo and Julia?' The cartoon of Romeo is saying 'wie ist die welt so schon' and Juliet replies 'ich liebe dich!' Mary accompanied Lavery on various trips as his model, but Lavery was well aware of how such a relationship could be construed.[43] In his autobiography he describes a trip they made to Brittany in 1904: 'taking with me "Spring", the little German girl, and Shiel, an Irishman with nothing to do. After working all day from a model in the country it has always been a relief to me to have a third person, male or female, to take the sitter off my hands, so to speak . . . Shiel served my purpose in that he shared the scandal, if there should be one, of my taking a beautiful girl to the country for months at a time.'[44]

60
An Arab Raid
c.1888
Watercolour heightened with
bodycolour on paper,
29.6×41.3
The Burrell Collection

Mary was the model for many of Lavery's paintings: *Mary in Green* (Ottawa, Canada); *The Lady in a Green Coat* (Bradford); *Mary with Roses* (Johannesburg); and *Spring* (pl 58). Never intended as portraits, these works aimed to delight the eye. Through Lavery Mary was befriended by Crawhall and was the lucky recipient of marvellous illustrated letters from him. Writing from his home at Brandsby, near Easingwold in Yorkshire, Crawhall says 'My dear Mary, I fear that there is but little chance of my accompanying you, Eileen and President to Morocco. I should have liked nothing better. You will enjoy yourself. You can stick pigs . . . I will perhaps see you before you start at least I hope so. Best Regards, yours ever, Foxcatcher.' In another letter he asks if she has ever ridden a camel (pl 57).

During one of his visits to his villa in Tangier, Lavery relates that his 'daughter and Mary accompanied me, and little did I dream that the latter was destined to remain in that country. Often attending the local sport of pig-sticking and polo she made the acquaintance of one Nigel d'Albini Black-Hawkins, who, after serving in South Africa with the Mounted Infantry during the Boer War, had settled down in North Africa. Before my return to England Mary and Nigel were married in the cathedral in Gibraltar. So Mary remained in Morocco, where she has taken a keen and useful interest in Moorish art, and in later years has given several private exhibitions of leather-work specially designed for her by native craftsmen.'[45] 'How Crawhall Pictured a Friend in the Boer War' (pl 59) is probably a caricature of Mary's husband.

Bearing in mind that Lavery and other close friends purchased property in Tangier, why was it then that Crawhall did not return there after 1893? In 1894 his father's health was giving serious cause for concern and it is possible that Crawhall chose to remain in England to be near his family. His sister Elspeth Challoner suggested that the reason was that he could not stand the spectacle of human heads being brought into the town on the top of spears. There can be no doubt that it was a violent country with warring tribesmen, bribery, corruption and the eternal problem of taxes.[46] An Arab Raid (pl 60) could be Crawhall's record of the fight between the Riff tribe and the Sultan's askari mentioned in Denholm Armour's Bridle and Brush.[47] Lavery also describes the violence of the country: 'The Moorish prison in Tangier is a kind of show-place where visitors are allowed to look through a hole in the door into an open courtyard where poor wretches are chained up like dogs in a kennel. There are no kind of sanitary arrangements, nor is there food and drink other than what their friends bring in, but they are allowed to work at baskets, mats etc. Eyes are put out, hands are cut off, and other tortures are inflicted, and the Moor will face any of them saying that it is the will of God. . . .'[48]

From Tangier, Crawhall made the short boat trip to Gibraltar and to Algeciras in Spain. Although no documentation survives to indicate how often or for how long he made these trips it would be reasonable to assume that he travelled there for a few days each time he visited Tangier. Simultaneously fascinated and repelled by the spectacle of the Spanish bullfight, Melville, Lavery, Denholm Armour and Crawhall all worked on this subject in the years 1890–1. In Bridle and Brush, Denholm Armour describes his first experience of a bullfight during a trip to Algeciras with Crawhall as 'one of the most stirring spectacles I have ever seen, despite the horror that the horse part makes one feel . . . Crawhall afterwards painted a very fine picture of a picador and bull, and I did a watercolour drawing of the team of mules dragging out the dead bull. . . .'[49] Denholm Armour might well have been referring to either The Bullfight (pl 61) or The Bull Ring, Algeciras (pl 62). Although Crawhall, Melville and Denholm Armour in depicting bullfights share a remarkable similarity in composition and wash technique, Crawhall's watercolours better convey the feeling of movement and are rarely as descriptive as the works of his friends. The Bullfight (pl 63) is unusual in that Crawhall normally concentrates on the role of the picador and only rarely shows the matador. In most the dark mass of the bull dominates the centre of the scene, contrasting with the horse, the victim. Earlier writers claim that the spectacle was repulsive to Crawhall because of the sacrifice of the horse.[50] If Crawhall did

61
The Bullfight
c.1889–91
Watercolour heightened with
bodycolour on paper,
38.8×36.5
The Burrell Collection

experience intense emotion when watching the bullfight, it is not communicated in these works which can be read as detached and dispassionate records of movement and colour.

It is the Spanish bullfight that is depicted in Walton's portrait of Crawhall (pl 33). Inscribed 'Madrid 1884' it is likely that while the portrait was painted from life the canvases and the setting were imaginary. Crawhall is seen standing lazily, pipe in hand, leaning rather dangerously against a large stretcher around which a canvas is stretched. This canvas faces another, presumably leaning against the studio wall. This second canvas, partially visible on the left, depicts a bullfight. The canvases are life-size and this scale contributes to the enigma of this painting, which itself is tiny. The painting is a fitting homage to Crawhall, recording his love of movement and colour, and executed in a style which at that time was both influenced by him and an influence on him.

Crawhall's experience in Spain, and more crucially in Tangier, was to free him from the need to conform to the dictates of tradition. He systematically developed and expanded his watercolour technique to capture the movement, the character and the colour of the animals he loved. That this had been an important period in his life and art there can be no doubt.

62
The Bull Ring, Algeciras
1891
Watercolour on paper,
28.1×40.7
Robert Fleming Holdings
Ltd.

63
The Bullfight
c.1889
Watercolour on paper,
31.5×46.0
Private Collection

J. Crawhall
Algeciras. '91

J. Crawhall

CHAPTER

4

EXHIBITIONS, COLLECTORS

AND DEALERS

It was quite in keeping with the fitness of things artistic that the first
exhibition of the collected works of Mr Joseph Crawhall jnr. should be
held in Glasgow. For in this art centre, especially on the part of
those who support the new movement, much appreciation has been shown
for his work. The opportunity of seeing it had hitherto been
far too seldom afforded at our exhibitions, which have always
left both lovers of pictures and painters anxious for more.

David Martin reviewing Crawhall's first one-man
show in *The Studio*, September 1894[1]

Joseph Crawhall's art was not widely known during his lifetime. Working
only when the mood was upon him Crawhall was not prolific; at most there
are four hundred works extant. His drawings and watercolours were bought
by a small group of Scottish collectors almost the minute they left his easel.
These collectors were prepared to lend to exhibitions at home and abroad but it
was often the same works that were shown year after year. In addition, the
watercolours had to vie for attention with large oils in mixed exhibitions where
they were often relegated to side rooms or corridors. There was little opportunity
for the public to become familiar with his work and today the situation largely
remains the same with many works still in private hands. The Glasgow shipowner
Sir William Burrell (1861–1958) formed the largest collection of Crawhall's
work, one hundred and forty drawings and paintings purchased between the
1880s and 1952. Although no work by Crawhall entered a public collection

64
A Mallard Rising
c.1908
Gouache on linen,
53.0×44.5
Private Collection

during the artist's lifetime, Burrell's gift of his collection to the city of Glasgow in 1944 and the opening of the Burrell Collection in 1983 have given the opportunity for his work to reach a wider audience.

R. B. Cunninghame Graham wrote that most 'artists, even those of the first rank, produce their works with drops of blood wrung from the soul. "Creeps" [Crawhall], I feel sure, suffered no pangs of parturition, and I remember once, when someone said all art was difficult, he answered simply, without a trace of boastfulness, but in the tone of one who states a fact, "No, not at all." '[2] Crawhall is known, however, to have been so highly critical of his own work that he destroyed much of it. His obituarist in *The Times* lamented that 'the world has lost hundreds of drawings which can ill be spared.'[3] One Glasgow dealer recalled hearing his own father say that 'he quite well remembers him [Crawhall] tearing up one or two drawings he was not satisfied with.'[4] It is true to say that many artists destroy works that do not satisfy them and Keene wrote to Crawhall's father that the 'disposition he [Crawhall] seems to have of getting dissatisfied with his work shows he's a real artist, but try and get him to stick hard to his ideas and work 'em out to the bitter end!'[5] According to an article written in 1911 it was not only ill-conceived or unfinished works that Crawhall destroyed. In a fit of despair Crawhall pitched *The Aviary* (pl 106) into a wastepaper bin from which it was mercifully rescued by the dealer W. B. Paterson.[6] In his letters to the dealer Alexander Reid, Crawhall frequently refers to this practice: 'I thought you would be wondering why the drawings had not arrived, but the alterations in the size meant rather more than I expected but there is no fear of them. . . .'; 'I hope to be able to send you a magnum [*sic*] soon, I have two that have been on the stocks for some time but contrary to my usual custom I have not burnt them'; 'I have the drawings nearly complete ie, out of danger. . . .'[7]

Another contributing factor to the relative scarcity of works was Crawhall's unwillingness to follow a regular routine of work. Unlike his artist friends he never seems to have needed to earn from his art. But Lord Gleichen was surely a little wide of the mark when he claimed that 'Crawhall, a really brilliant young artist . . . handicapped by the possession of a rich aunt, only painted at intervals. . . .'[8] As no 'rich aunt' existed he may possibly have mistaken Crawhall's father for one. Crawhall senior had numerous business interests outside the family ropeworks and his account books record many and varied investments. His home and collection suggest a comfortable even an elegant existence and one biographer mentions the gilt buttons that belonged to the family's footman and butler, essential adjuncts for those who entertain.[9] Also in the letter quoted above Keene goes on to imply the existence of an allowance; 'You'll have to make him realise by keeping him short of money.'[10] When Crawhall senior retired from business and as his health declined, it is clear that he was concerned for the welfare of his artist son. In a letter to his sisters he comments on the lack of livelihood of Joseph, Hugh and Beatrice. 'I cannot afford to keep them idle as it comes hard upon me under my altered circumstances having no business to attend to.'[11] By 1894 Crawhall senior was busy arranging, through his son-in-law Frederick Challoner, that Challoner act as a trustee of a fund to take care of his son 'who earned money through his pictures but whose carelessness for the ordinary amenities of life along with the irregularity of his income from painting made some kind of more stable arrangement a necessity.'[12]

Although Crawhall never married and from the mid-1890s lived at home with his mother and youngest sister, it is clear from his correspondence with Alexander Reid that he not only needed money but was concerned that he was paid properly for his work. Crawhall evidently suggested a price for each work: 'I did not understand that this pony was to be thrown in with the other two, however if that was the arrangement I suppose it must stand . . . You can send me £50 of the £80 as soon as convenient as I am in need of some ready';[13] 'I was quite under the impression that I had sent you the price of the two drawings. What do you say to £100? I think the cock is fairly good . . . If you agree to the price you might send me on some of it as I am somewhat low in funds.'[14] On occasion Reid disputed the price and angry letters followed. On 19 November 1900 Crawhall writes: 'Many thanks for cheque, although I certainly think the price an absurd one, however, as you say you have a number, and I conclude don't want any more I must dispose of them elsewhere. I find I have been throwing my work away and I must say I don't think you have treated me quite fairly, as the prices I have received compared with the prices you get, are out of all character, however as you have raised the question it leaves me free to do the best for myself.'[15] A few days later Crawhall replies to a letter from Reid: 'to plunge at once in "media res" you say that "I have made the prices myself", remember you have repeatedly written to say that you can't give so much. The matter of slight drawings is rather difficult because I have so often found that I have accepted a low price for a drawing you considered slight, and afterwards been astonished to find that it has brought a better price than a finished one. However as you say you must have a profit on something which seems reasonable, and I have no wish to sell my work elsewhere provided, I get a fair price. . . .'[16]

Watercolours would not normally be expected to fetch the large sums of money that could be commanded by, for example, a portrait in oil. In 1898 Guthrie's fees were £200 for a quarter-length, £400 for a half-length and £650 for a full-length portrait.[17] Crawhall, by watercolour standards, and doubtless because of the scarcity of his works, always commanded good prices. At the time of his death in 1913 his estate was valued at £6,188 17s. 2d. By 1922 his works were changing hands for considerable sums. *The Jackdaw* (National Gallery of Victoria, Melbourne) sold in 1922 for £1,250 and in 1935 *A Mallard Rising* (pl 64) sold for £1,207 10s.

Most artists, as today, had to have their work exhibited to attract the attention of potential patrons. Crawhall, like the other Glasgow Boys, exhibited in local

65
The Black Rabbit
c.1894
Gouache on linen,
23.5×33.7
Paul Mellon Collection,
Upperville, Virginia

66
The Magpie
c.1906
Gouache on linen,
30.3×43.5
The Burrell Collection

67
Pigeons on the Roof
c.1895
Gouache on linen,
40.5×35.0
The Burrell Collection

Glasgow exhibitions and in provincial shows throughout Britain, and was a member of three exhibiting bodies: the Scottish (becoming the Royal Scottish in 1888) Society of Painters in Watercolours from 1887 to 1893, the International Society of Sculptors, Painters and Gravers from 1898 to 1913 and the New English Art Club from 1909 to 1913. But by 1894 most of his pictures were sold privately and so exhibitions had to draw on loans and did not have any of his work to sell. This frustrated interested buyers as much as the art critics who perpetually complained of the limited chance to see his work and the even rarer opportunities to buy.

From 1878 to 1881 Crawhall exhibited works at the spring and autumn exhibitions of the Newcastle Arts Association. These early works were for sale for around £10 but whether they found a purchaser or not is not known. Guthrie and Walton had also contributed to these exhibitions, taking advantage of their friendship with Crawhall. They in turn persuaded Crawhall to send to the various Glasgow venues. The Glasgow Institute of the Fine Arts was the chief exhibiting and selling vehicle open to the Glasgow Boys who had met with a hostile reception in their early attempts to exhibit at the Royal Scottish Academy. It was at the Glasgow Institute of the Fine Arts that the local industrialists came to furnish their houses and young artists came to study the foreign and British loan sections. Of the total of nineteen works by Crawhall shown at the Glasgow Institute, nine were exhibited during his lifetime, of which only two were for sale: *Disappointment* (£10) in 1882 and a *Cloot Drain, Lincolnshire* (£12 12s) in 1883. From 1883 until 1895 no work by Crawhall appeared at the Glasgow Institute. Although it is possible that he sent works which were rejected it is more likely that he had found in the Scottish Society of Painters in Watercolours, also based in Glasgow, a more suitable venue. When from now on his pictures were shown at the Institute they were works borrowed from local collectors: in 1895 George Burrell (William's brother) lent *The Circus* (pl 110) and *The Black Rabbit* (pl 65); in 1903 John Nairn lent *The Piebald* (Private Collection); in 1905 J. A. Holms lent *Pigeons on the Roof* (pl 67) and *Jackdaw with Peacock's Feathers* and John Keppie lent *The Farmer's Boy* (possibly pl 35); in 1909 a Mr Archibald Robertson lent *The Bull Ring* and in 1913, after Crawhall's death, W. A. Coats lent *The Magpie* (pl 66) and *The White Drake* (pl 68) and Lady Smiley *A Huntsman* (Private Collection).

On 19 December 1877, the art critic 'Megilp' of Glasgow's satirical weekly magazine *The Bailie* informed his readers that Mr William Smith of the Glasgow Institute intended calling a meeting to discuss the setting up of a watercolour society in Glasgow, 'such a society is much required here. . . .'[18] By 26 December he was writing that as the Society should represent the whole of Scotland the co-operation of Edinburgh artists was being sought. The Scottish Society of Painters in Watercolours was founded in 1878.[19] Although not one of the Glasgow Boys was among the original twenty-five members, in 1885 when the Society held an open exhibition three Glasgow Boys were elected to membership:

68
The White Drake
c.1895
Gouache on linen,
40.7×57.1
Private Collection

69
The Black Cock
c.1894
Gouache on linen,
39.3×51.1
The Burrell Collection

Arthur Melville, James Paterson and E. A. Walton.[20] In 1886 the membership, previously limited to forty, became unlimited, in order to augment funds but also to cope with the increasing interest in and demands upon the Society. Applicants for membership had to submit two watercolours for inspection. The success of the Society is recorded in a Minute of 26 January 1887: one hundred and one works (from six hundred and eighty-nine) were purchased from the 1886 exhibition. The sum of £234 8s. had been taken in admission money and £1,425 9s. in purchases. There was actually a decrease of £61 17s. in admission receipts and this 'must', according to the Minute, 'be attributed to the continued commercial and industrial depression.' Six artists were proposed for membership in the same Minute, one of whom was Joseph Crawhall junior of 2 Sydenham Terrace, Newcastle upon Tyne. Crawhall, not surprisingly, was proposed by Walton and seconded by one Duncan Mackellar. That there was at least one objection to Crawhall's election is seen in the Minutes of the Special General Meeting held on 16 February 1887. When William McTaggart suggested that all six candidates be elected Mr Smart asked if membership was restricted to 'Scotchmen artists resident in

Scotland'. The Secretary replied that no such understanding had ever existed and all six were duly elected. Crawhall was a member of the Society from 1887 until 1893 when, at a Special General Meeting in the Bath Hotel, 152 Bath Street, on Tuesday, 19 December, 'The Secretary ... intimated the resignation of Mr Crawhall and said that Messrs John Macdougall and Arthur Melville who were considerably in arrears with their subscriptions had failed to pay and had been struck off the roll of membership. . . .' Crawhall's period of membership co-incided with the period of his closest association with the Glasgow Boys; with his move from oil to watercolour and specifically with the production of his Tangier watercolours, most of which were seen at the Society's exhibitions for the first time. Unlike the Glasgow Institute of the Fine Arts Crawhall clearly used the Scottish Society of Painters in Watercolours as a selling venue.

In 1886 he exhibited three works.[21] *A White Horse* (twelve guineas) might be *Barb Horse in Stable* (pl 47) purchased by William Burrell at the exhibition at the same time as the artist, James Whitelaw Hamilton, purchased *The Duckpond* at eight guineas (pl 25). At the Tenth Annual Exhibition of the Scottish Society of Painters in Watercolours, held at the Institute galleries at 175 Sauchiehall Street in 1887, Crawhall exhibited a minimum of nine works. These included *A Pasture near the Sea* at ten guineas, which can possibly be identified as *Sheep in a Meadow* (pl 38), *The Forge* at £22 10s. (pl 32) and *Left in Charge* at twelve guineas. From descriptions of *Left in Charge* in the reviews of the exhibition it is possible to identify it as *The Byre* (pl 29). But it is not clear what the 'Illustrations' at £30 were although they may have been drawings of deer or of pig-sticking. A lengthy paragraph on Crawhall's art was included in the review of the exhibition which appeared in the *Glasgow Herald* on 4 November. 'Joseph Crawhall, a young artist from Newcastle-on-Tyne, bids fair to come rapidly to the front. He is represented this year by nine drawings, all of them notable for their defects and their excellences. His method is imperfect, yet the effects which he gets show executive skill of highest promise. He is not careful of form. Of this we have an example in *Garden Path* n.171 a small sketch chiefly made up of what seems to be a confused mingling of Chinese characters. He stops where it might be easy to go on to the finish, as in *Left in Charge* n.95, a boyish cow-tender, who leans, a mere lay-figure, against the wall. Yet, in all his drawings there is admirable tone and unmistakeable grip. Take *The Forge* n.184 and, in the horse, with its extremely difficult foreshortening, you see how accurate is his draughtsmanship, in the sheen of the animal's dark hide how subleties are successfully caught, and in the inner blaze of the forge, how the activities of the farrier are realised in a way that few young artists could rival. His *Pigeons* n.216 is a little gem of colour, whilst in *Harriers* n.145 dogs at rest and in all stages of sleepiness, his bold, rapid handling is redeemed by its effectiveness.'[22]

At the Eleventh Annual Exhibition of the Royal Scottish Society of Painters in Watercolours (RSW) Crawhall exhibited seven works, all for sale and all of

Tangier subjects, including *A Moorish Packhorse* (pl 46), *The Snake Charmer* (pl 44), which was bought by George Burrell, and *Camels* (pl 49). The *Scottish Art Review* carried a review of the exhibition by the artist George Henry, who concluded that 'the average merit of the exhibition is not high.' Henry approved of the 'general effect of the rooms [which] has been made very pleasant by a skilful scheme of decoration. Above the pictures is a frieze of grey canvas, stamped with a design, rich and bold in form, and most simple and artistic in effect.' He deplored the hanging, which had been carried out by Melville, Nisbet and Laing. 'Neither in point of harmonious effect, decorative scheme, balance of colour, nor in the matter of dealing strict justice to the exhibitors, have they accomplished all that could be desired with the materials they had in hand. In the case of Mr Crawhall's work this is specially noticeable, as his pictures are unquestionably amongst the finest in the exhibition, and in some cases they have been hung in positions where they cannot be seen to advantage.' He continues, 'of Mr Joseph Crawhall's work, the most important and in some respects the finest, *The Snake-Charmer*, n.218, is hung so high that it is almost impossible except for an artist to see and appreciate its peculiar beauties. In the particular phase of art expression in which Mr Crawhall is best known, viz. the artistic realisation of animal life, though lacking somewhat in reserve force, yet, nothing equal to his work can be found in England to-day. His subtle analysis of characterisation, keen accuracy of drawing, and perfect mastery of methods, renders his work quite unique. Any of his drawings will suffice as an example. Note in them the originality of composition, the sense of decorative quality, the charm of colour, the range and harmony of tones, the knowledge of exactly what to do, and where to do it, combined with intelligence and deftness in the treatment.'[23]

A rather different assessment of Crawhall's contribution is to be found in the review of the exhibition in the *Glasgow Herald* on 28 November: 'What shall we say in this connection of the works of Joseph Crawhall, jun, a young artist who surprises and disappoints us by turns. We have spoken of Mr Crawhall's work in other exhibitions as we felt – that is to say, with frank recognition of his cleverness and dash. But these are talents which may be misused, especially when they are bestowed on a young artist. On the present occasion, Mr Crawhall is disappointing. His *Moorish Donkeys* n.274 are formless and chaotic. His *Snake Charmer, Morocco* n.218 will charm no-one, whether of reptilian or human kind. Art cannot be reduced to a mere vague suggestion, and Mr Crawhall's sketches are nothing more.'

In 1889 two Algeciras bullfight scenes by Crawhall were for sale and *The Aviary, Clifton* (pl 106) was lent by the dealer W. B. Paterson. Crawhall had three works, none of which were for sale, in the 1891 exhibition reviewed in the *Glasgow Herald* on 6 November. 'The exhibition in connection with the Royal Society of Painters in Water-Colours was carried last year to London. We are not sure how far this experiment justified itself financially, but on the higher ground of

70
The Pigeon
c.1894
Gouache on linen,
25.7×32.2
The Burrell Collection

71
The Spangled Cock
c.1903
Gouache on linen,
44.5×58.4
Paul Mellon Collection,
Upperville, Virginia

showing how this peculiarly British form of art has been carried in Scotland, it was undoubtedly successful. Those who diligently make the rounds of London galleries have been educated, in this and other ways, out of the belief that no good things can come from the North. The experiment from this point of view was well worth making, but a repetition was unnecessary, and, accordingly, the Society has arranged its Fourteenth Annual Exhibition in the Institute Galleries, Sauchiehall Street.' A smaller exhibition than usual, with only two hundred works (as compared to two hundred and eighty-three in 1888), it had in the opinion of the reviewer 'reached a higher level of pure art – a growing tendency to paint with a freer hand . . . without any sacrifice to refinement.' Once again Crawhall is singled out for comment: 'Joseph Crawhall has some sketches in white frames which, for that reason, we presume, have been hung in the entrance hall. They are bright and spirited to a degree and would only lose in effectiveness by any attempt to carry the execution further.'[24]

The Sixteenth Annual Exhibition of the Society was held at the Royal Academy, National Galleries, Edinburgh. *The Studio*'s reviewer commented that it 'may safely be said that the National Galleries are the most adaptable in Scotland for picture shows. In two of the rooms the walls are draped with neutral yellow, the other two in a red brown, with appropriate friezes.' Once more Crawhall had three works on show of which one, *A Hound Asleep* (Glasgow Art Gallery and Museum) was for sale. Both *The Circus* (pl 110) and *Bullfight at Algeciras* (possibly pl 61) were on loan – quite probably from the collections of George and William Burrell. *The Studio*'s critic wrote that the 'drawings of Mr Joe Crawhall are always interesting, and to the art student especially so, as they show remarkable technical qualities and correct draughtsmanship – in fact, the work of a painter who thoroughly understands what he is painting. *The Bullfight, Algeciras*, is his best. It has fine drawing, good though reserved colour scheme, and is particularly virile in execution.'[25]

Just as Crawhall had been introduced to the RSW by his Glasgow friends, notably Walton, it was undoubtedly through them that he became an executive member of the council of the London-based International Society of Sculptors, Painters and Gravers. This new Society had been the brainchild of Francis Howard who intended that it should have Whistler as chairman. Howard recognised the need for an exhibiting body prepared to show the works of avant-garde artists and which would invite continental artists to contribute on a regular basis. In addition paintings and sculpture were to be displayed together in well-lit galleries where works could be carefully hung with sufficient space rather than, as was traditional, uncomfortably crowded. At the first meeting of the Society on 23 December 1897 Howard was joined by Crawhall's Glasgow Boy friends Walton and John Lavery. In February 1898 a list of artists who would be invited to contribute was drawn up and it included the names of Glasgow Boy artists Paterson, Melville, Henry, Hornel, Whitelaw Hamilton and Crawhall. By the time of the Society's thirteenth meeting on 4 May 1898 Crawhall had already been elected to the executive council and was present for the election of office-bearers. Whistler was elected as President, having been proposed by Lavery and seconded by Shannon, and Lavery was elected as Vice-President, proposed by Walton and seconded by Crawhall. At the fifteenth meeting on 16 December 1898 Crawhall proposed that artists, when receiving invitations to send to the exhibition, should also receive guarantee forms with a note appended explaining their function (raising capital by selling shares). Crawhall's motion was seconded by Howard. These shares were necessary to help secure the financial stability of the Society and both Crawhall and his mother are recorded as guarantors in 1899: 'Margaret B. Crawhall Beacon Banks, Easingwold, Yorks, £50; Jos. Crawhall as above, £50.' In March 1901 they both gave a further £25 each. Another guarantor, presumably wishing to encourage his Glasgow Boy contacts, was one 'William Burrell of 54 George Square, £25.' Even the briefest perusal of the Society's minutes, however, shows that Crawhall, unlike Lavery, Walton and Guthrie, rarely attended the Council meetings. These weekly meetings held in London would have been impossible for the now Yorkshire-based Crawhall to attend.[26]

Crawhall attended meetings on 3 and 25 May 1899 but was not present again until five years later on 27 May and 7 and 15 July 1904. After Whistler's death in 1903 the French sculptor Rodin was elected President and Crawhall was present at the meeting on 21 February 1905 when Rodin was in the chair. Crawhall attended further meetings on 6 March and 7 December 1905 and on 26 February, 22 November and 18 December 1906. At the meeting held on 24 September 1913 at the Grosvenor Gallery 'The Honorary Secretary reported that Mr Walton had communicated to him that the Crawhall collection would not be ready for the forthcoming exhibition, and proposed holding it to the Spring.'

Crawhall's role was not an important one, even on the few occasions when he did attend. Macaulay Stevenson's letter to John Lavery, written after Whistler's death and referring to the vacant executive posts on the International Society Council is to be read with a pinch of salt: 'Now John this thing should be done right. You as President and Joe Crawhall as vice. (You've both had a fair training in vice). Seriously, John, I think this would be first the right men in the right place.'[27]

The Society's stated aim was 'to hold exhibitions of the finest art of the day. . . .' It had no particular artistic axe to grind but was against the monopolistic practices of the Royal Academy. The first exhibition in 1898 was held in Prince's Skating Rink, Knightsbridge. The main hall was divided into three galleries, decorated with canvas painted French grey. The glass roof was screened with white muslin and below this a velarium of dark grey muslin was suspended. The paintings were hung two deep. There were two hundred and fifty-six exhibitors at this first exhibition including Manet, Degas and Whistler. The *Glasgow Evening Citizen* said that the 'character of the show may be described as French-cum-Glasgow-

72
*Cock Pheasant with Foliage
and Berries*
c.1906
*Gouache on linen,
36.5×61.0*
Private Collection

cum-Whistler. . . .'[28] Crawhall was represented by seven works including *The Black Cock* (pl 69), *The Pigeon* (pl 70), *Performing Dogs* (probably pl 110) and *The Black Rabbit* (pl 65) which, along with works by Puvis de Chavannes, were hung in the south gallery. 'Crawhall's seven exhibits, although small and in water or bodycolour on silk or paper, typified the qualities to which many of the artists showing aspired: fine drawings, a low colour key, rarefied tonality, and a decorative, and "poetic" sensibility.'[29] Crawhall is mentioned in most of the many reviews of the exhibition.[30] 'I am not sure whether Mr Crawhall hails from the Northern City, but from his work I should say he does. His sketches of animals are simply marvellous, and if it be true that they are done from memory they are more wonderful still. The drawings exhibited here are done in watercolour on canvas, *The Black Cock* and *The Pigeon* are well nigh perfect. . . .'[31] The reviewer in the *St. Paul's Magazine*, while praising *The Black Cock*, had strong reservations about other works: 'In *The Black Rabbit*, and also *The Huntsman* beside it, I felt some of the dangers of the method, and a suspicion of weakness in the artist – a certain thinness and feebleness. So marked a technique has always a danger of a missed effect hovering upon its craftsmanship. But what can be done by so accomplished an artist, with an instrument under his full control, can only be realised by looking at *The Black Cock* and *The Doves*.'[32]

In 1899 Crawhall was represented by four works including *Huntsmen and Hounds* (identified from an illustrated catalogue as pl 123), *A Horse Fair* (again identified from the catalogue as pl 111) and by William Burrell's *The Bullfight* (pl 61). Crawhall exhibited two works at the third exhibition in 1901 and only one, *The Spangled Cock* (pl 71), at the fourth exhibition in 1904. *The Athenaeum*'s critic described it as a 'brilliant drawing, delightful for its certainty and directness of touch.'[33] At the seventh exhibition, held in the New Gallery from January to March 1907, Crawhall exhibited four works including *The Magpie* (pl 66), *Cock Pheasant with Foliage and Berries* (pl 72) and *The White Drake* (pl 68). *A Mallard Rising* (pl 64) and *The Circus Rider* (Burrell Collection) were in the ninth exhibition in 1909. At the International Society's *Century of Art* exhibition at the Grafton Galleries in June and July of 1911 *The Magpie* and *The Spangled Cock* were once more on view and were Crawhall's last contributions to the Society's exhibitions during his lifetime.

The New English Art Club (NEAC) was founded in 1886. In its early days it consisted of a varied group of young artists such as Tuke, Wilson Steer, Stanhope Forbes and Clausen of the Newlyn school and quite a number of the Glasgow Boys, Lavery and Walton being the first two Glasgow painters to associate

73
The Chinese Goose
c.1905
Gouache on linen,
32.0×41.0
The Burrell Collection

themselves with the group, both appearing in its second exhibition in 1887. These artists shared similar influences; most were Paris-trained and had been influenced by Bastien-Lepage. Alfred Thornton said of the NEAC that it 'has been the chief nursery or kindergarten of the fresh talents disclosed in the half-century of its activity. . . . Into a hothouse of sentimentality in the late '80s it blew again the fresh breath of the open air, of the vitality of the thing seen, of reality faced and its beauty sought out.'[34] Increasing importance, due to the dominance of Brown and Tonks, was given to drawing and watercolour. Until 1913 the NEAC abided by its original constitution limiting the number of members' works, and retaining a strict jury system. There was free admission, however, for outsiders when they were judged worthy of being invited.

Crawhall did not exhibit at the NEAC in the early years when the Glasgow Boys were there in force. Although he exhibited in 1890 alongside Guthrie, Henry, Lavery, Walton and Alexander Mann, he was represented by *In the Parrot House*, now *The Aviary* (pl 106), which had however been included in many other exhibitions in that year. His Glasgow friends resigned *en masse* in 1893, seemingly over some dispute about one of their number being rejected.[35] Crawhall only became a member in 1909 and remained one until his death. As with the International Society exhibitions Crawhall was represented at the NEAC with works drawn from private collections which in most instances had already been exhibited elsewhere. In 1909 he showed ten works in all, six at the summer exhibition and four in the winter. They included *The Magpie* (pl 66), *Cock Pheasant with Foliage and Berries* (pl 72), *The Chinese Goose* (pl 73), *French Cab Horse* (pl 21) and *The Rook's Nest* (pl 74). He was not an active member as he was only to show one work each in the summer of 1910 and the winter of 1912.

Apart from the pictures shown in the London and Glasgow exhibitions works by Crawhall were seen in exhibitions in Paisley, Dundee and Liverpool; at the international exhibitions in Glasgow in 1888 and 1901; and at various London galleries – the Grosvenor (1890 and 1912), the Grafton (1893 and 1894) and the Whitechapel Art Gallery (1901, 1907 and 1910).

Two dealers specialised in handling and exhibiting the works of Joseph Crawhall – Alexander Reid (1854–1928) and W. B. Paterson (1859–1952). Two retrospective exhibitions of his work were held during his lifetime: one at the Glasgow gallery of Alexander Reid in 1894 and the other at the London gallery of William Bell Paterson in 1912. In both exhibitions, however, most of the works were on loan from private collections.

William Burrell believed that Alexander Reid had done 'more than any other man has ever done to introduce fine pictures to Scotland and to create a love of art.'[36] Reid's gallery, La Société des Beaux-Arts, established in 1889, 'introduced many new and unfamiliar pictures to Scotland, acted as a focus of discussion for artists, collectors and critics, and quietly effected a revolution in taste.' Reid 'brought to art dealing a passionate commitment which meant that the affluent

74
The Rook's Nest
c.1908
Gouache on linen,
56.2×43.7
The Burrell Collection

75
Huntsman Taking a Toss
c.1894
Chalk and watercolour on
paper, 34.3×29.2
Robert Fleming Holdings
Ltd.

mercantile classes of Glasgow couldn't afford to ignore works of art. He cared about the artist, and about the works that he handled. He nurtured many a collector, helping them to dispose of their early and often worthless acquisitions and leading them to works of greater significance.'[37]

Reid initially specialised in the works of Dutch and Barbizon artists. He was the eldest son of James G. Reid who in 1857 had founded the firm of Kay and Reid, carvers and gilders. By the 1870s they were the leading firm in Glasgow with some eighty employees. In 1877 Reid was given a room in which to show paintings and he was soon showing works by the Glasgow Boys and Crawhall. In 1887 Reid travelled to Paris where he was introduced to the work of the Impressionists and

Post-Impressionists by Theo van Gogh and for a short time shared lodgings with Theo's brother Vincent. It was as a result of this training that in the early 1890s he brought works by Degas, Monet, Pissarro and Sisley into Scotland. From 1892 he was also in correspondence with Whistler. Throughout he continued to show the work of the Glasgow Boys. It was Reid who accompanied Guthrie to Munich in September 1890 to assist with the preparations for the Glasgow Boys' participation, and who was responsible for most of the arrangements for the exhibition at St Louis in 1895. Reid's relationship with the artists of the Glasgow school was never purely one of business. He helped, encouraged and befriended them and the existence of sketches such as *Huntsman Taking a Toss* (pl 75) points to the close nature of the friendship between Crawhall and Reid.

After his return from Paris, Reid moved into premises in West George Street in Glasgow and then in 1894 to larger, more accessible premises at 124 St Vincent Street. It was in these new premises in April 1894 that the Crawhall exhibition took place. There were eighty works listed in the published *Catalogue of the Collected Works of Jos. Crawhall, Jr.* which included a short essay on the artist by Reid (see Appendix Two). This exhibition according to Reid contained 'the bulk of his life-work'. Most of the works were on loan from private collectors who, unfortunately, are listed at the end of the catalogue rather than beside the works they had lent. The lenders included T. G. Arthur, George and William Burrell, James Gardiner, John Keppie and J. J. Spencer.

From surviving correspondence between Reid and Crawhall we know that the artist had agreed to Reid having a monopoly of the sale of his work in Scotland. In a letter written in November 1900 Crawhall complained that as Reid was offering ludicrously low prices simply because he had a number of his works in stock, he was threatening to take his works elsewhere. In his next letter, though, Crawhall writes: 'I have no wish to sell my work elsewhere provided, I get a fair price. . . .'[38] Crawhall, now based in Yorkshire, depended upon Reid for assistance in securing loans from private collectors for the many exhibitions he participated in at the turn of the century. In 1901 Crawhall, needing to secure loans for the International Society's third exhibition, writes, 'I want to know if you can get me two pictures to exhibit at the International. I should like the *White Duck* and the *Horses on the Hill* that Arthur has you know the two. . . .'[39] Such negotiations were not always simple, especially when the same collectors were continually being asked to part with favourite works for months at a time. In his next letter Crawhall sympathises with Reid: 'I am sorry the "duck" owner is such a badger certainly don't run any risk of insult again. If you can get Arthur's it will do quite well, Burrell's horse fair was shown last time.' This same letter reveals Crawhall's opinion of these exhibitions for he continues: 'I am quite of your opinion that showing is not of any great use to me, but this is exceptional as I think the show mostly of support, I promised to contribute when possible.'[40] Crawhall felt himself obliged to show and consequently warned Reid that works must be made available to him. Referring to a recently finished 'Cock' he writes, 'it is a drawing I am rather fond of, and mind don't sell it to anyone who objects to let you have it to exhibit if you think of having a show next year.'[41]

In the 1894 exhibition catalogue Reid writes, 'The works of Crawhall have long been the exquisite delight of his brother artists, and of a public which, though necessarily restricted as the supply, has been found among the aristocracy of art amateurs – among those who may truly be called men of taste.' It was Alexander Reid who sold the works of Crawhall to these 'men of taste', T. G. Arthur, George and William Burrell, J. A. Holms, Leonard Gow and W. A. Coats.

One of Reid's clients was Thomas Glen Arthur (1858–1907). The second son of James Arthur of Paisley, Arthur was a director in the family firm, Arthur & Co., a major Glasgow company 'at the head of the Scottish trade in Textile Manufacturers and all allied departments, there was no other House whose commercial relations and connections were of stronger established or more widely extended influence.'[42] Arthur was the leading Scottish collector of Dutch and French pictures in the late 1880s and early 1890s, buying works by Maris, Bosboom, Boudin and Fantin-Latour from Reid and from Craibe Angus. One of the earliest collectors of Crawhall's work, he also succeeded in persuading the artist to accept a commission for ten drawings illustrating the tale of *Reynard the Fox* (pls 95–104). The subject was entirely appropriate for artist and collector shared a passion for hunting and Arthur no doubt invited Crawhall to ride from his stables at his home, Carrick House.

Like Arthur, the brothers George (1857–1927) and William (1861–1958) Burrell were major lenders to Reid's 1894 exhibition. Partners in the shipowning firm Burrell and Son, they shared an interest in the fine arts and in the work of Joseph Crawhall. *The Snake Charmer* (pl 44) and *The Bullfight* (pl 63) were purchased by George Burrell directly from the RSW but *The Circus* (pl 110) and *The Black Rabbit* (pl 65) probably came through Reid's hands. Although purchasing major examples of Crawhall's work, George never tried to form a comprehensive collection of the artist's work in the way his brother William was to do. In an article in *The Studio* in 1922 on William Burrell's collection of Crawhalls 'T.C.M.' wrote: 'If you were to offer Mr Burrell a Degas, a Monticelli, or a Matthew Maris, he would probably ponder long before deciding to purchase. He would have it sent home for a few days, examined in different lights, perhaps even hung on his walls, and seriously discussed and considered. And then would come the decision, for or against. But if you offered him a Crawhall he would succumb at once.'[43] In 1924 a considerable portion of Burrell's collection of paintings, including works by Crawhall, was on loan to the Tate in London. These works remained on loan for many years but, in 1927, Burrell writes to the Director 'I find I can hang some pictures here and wish eventually all the Crawhalls.'[44] Spurning Degas and Manet, Burrell requested the Crawhalls for his home Hutton Castle at Berwick-on-Tweed.

William Burrell might have met Crawhall in Reid's gallery or through the artist's friend John Lavery. Burrell seemingly invited Crawhall to dinner, 'the artist ate a hearty meal then fell asleep until very late, when he had to be sent off in a cab.'[45] What Burrell made of this has not been recorded, but in his nineties he 'was still speaking with enthusiasm of "Young Joe"'.[46] From 1911 Burrell kept a series of books recording his purchases and from these it is known that from 1916 until 1952 he acquired one hundred and twenty-five works by the artist. Loans and exhibition reviews confirm that Burrell was purchasing as early as 1890 and as a number of works by Crawhall in the Burrell Collection are not listed in the purchase books they must have been acquired prior to 1911 – these include *The Aviary* (pl 106), *The Black Cock* (pl 69) and *The Pigeon* (pl 70). Burrell also collected Crawhall's father's books. His copy of *A Jubilee Thought* is inscribed 'Wm. Burrell/Jany 1893' and *Olde ffrendes* 'Wm. Burrell/1895'. He owned copies of the second edition of *The Compleatest Angling Booke*, *Chap-book Chaplets* and *Impresses Quaint*. Today housed in the Burrell Collection, William Burrell's collection of the works of Joseph Crawhall is the largest and finest extant.

William Burrell's friend Robert Lorimer was the architect responsible for Formakin in Renfrewshire, the home of another early collector of Crawhall's work. Like T. G. Arthur, the wealthy Glasgow stockbroker John Augustus Holms (1866–1938) shared Crawhall's love of hunting. At the turn of the century Holms bought three important works from Alexander Reid: *The Jackdaw* (National Gallery of Victoria, Melbourne) in January 1902 for £95; *The Spangled Cock* (pl 71) in September 1902 for £160 and *Pigeons on the Roof* (pl 67) in October 1904 for £110. Holms also collected Chinese porcelain, English silver plate, Oriental rugs and English furniture and, although some items from his collection eventually passed into Burrell's hands, of the three Crawhalls only *Pigeons on the Roof* did.

The Spangled Cock eventually entered the collection of D. W. T. Cargill (d.1939) whose family had founded the Burmah Oil Company. Cargill had a magnificent collection of works by the Impressionists and Post-Impressionists, a collection unfortunately dispersed after his death. Cargill bought extensively from Reid from 1918 until 1938, including works by Monet, Degas, Van Gogh and Gauguin. In 1923 he bought five small Crawhalls from Reid for £380, one of which was *The Rabbits* (pl 86). Further Crawhall purchases were made in 1923 and in May 1930.[47]

Another important early collector of works by Crawhall and a friend of both Holms and Burrell was Leonard Gow (1859–1936). Gow was a senior partner in the firm Gow, Harrison and Company, shipowners, brokers, insurance agents and coal exporters who by 1912 were managing a fleet of seventeen high-class cargo-steamers. Harrison and Gow were both interested collectors and T. J. Honeyman observed: 'Whenever I looked in at the office in Gordon Street I seemed always to be interrupting talks on Art, not on shipping.'[48] Although Gow had a collection of Old Master paintings the strength of his collection lay in works of the French nineteenth century. Gow was buying from Reid from 1911 until 1928 and is known to have purchased works by Crawhall in 1922 and 1928.[49] Gow owned Crawhall's *In the Park* (pl 125), *Woman at Races* (pl 113) and, after Cargill, *The Rabbits* (pl 86). His love of hunting is seen in his ownership too of *Following the Hounds* (pl 121) and *Feathering the Line* (Private Collection).

One of the few collectors who could rival William Burrell in the passionate acquisition of works by Crawhall was William Allen Coats (1853–1926). Coats was a partner in the thread manufacturing firm of J. and P. Coats of Paisley which occupied a dominant place in the textile industry. Coats was an important client of Alexander Reid, purchasing works by Boudin, Monticelli, Géricault, Jongkind and Bosboom from him in the period between 1899 and 1911. In April 1907 he is known to have purchased two works by Crawhall, one of which was *The Sportsman's Dream (on the Eve of the 12th)* (pl 112) for £20, and he purchased *The Circus* in June 1907 for £165. *The Circus* was included in the 1927 Coats sale and was purchased for William Burrell for the sum of £750 by W. B. Paterson.

Sadly, detailed records of Coats' purchases no longer exist. *Cock Pheasant with Foliage and Berries* (pl 72) and *A Mallard Rising* (pl 64) were lent by Coats to the Rome International Fine Arts Exhibition in 1911; he lent *The Magpie* (pl 66) to Liverpool in 1912; *The White Drake* (pl 68) to the Royal Glasgow Institute of the Fine Arts in 1913; and *A Trout Rising* (pl 76) to Liverpool in 1922. In 1927 the forty-six works by Crawhall that formed Coats' collection were exhibited at W. B. Paterson's gallery in Suffolk Street in London. Some of the works were for sale and, through Paterson, William Burrell purchased *The Circus*, *Lady on Horseback* and *The Magpie*. The remaining works passed to Coats' sons Thomas Heywood Coats of Nitshill and Major John A. Coats of Dundonald who continued to allow them to be included in many exhibitions.

At the Christie's sale of W. A. Coats' sons' collections in London on Friday, 12 April 1935, most of what remained of W. A. Coats' Crawhall collection was dispersed. Twenty-seven works by Crawhall figured in the part of the sale devoted to the late Major J. A. Coats' collection. The sale attracted extensive press coverage. C. R. Carter, writing in the *Daily Telegraph* on 13 March, alerted prospective purchasers: 'Whistler held his [Crawhall] water-colour drawings to be masterpieces of observation. Recently the sale-room has supported this opinion, and last year a vivid Crawhall drawing of a scene near Tangier fetched £400 . . . A big opportunity, therefore, is to be offered to the collecting world on April 12 at Christie's, when the late Major J. A. Coats's share of his father's art possessions, containing as many as 27 superb works by the Newcastle artist, will be offered.'

Carter then reviews the sale itself in an article entitled: 'CRAWHALL OF NEWCASTLE – AUCTION TRIUMPH AT CHRISTIE'S.' He records that a series of Crawhall's 'remarkably graphic drawings evoked the most enthusiastic bouts of bidding, culminating in one of 1,150 gs for the subject of a mallard rising from the

76
A Trout Rising
c.1907
Gouache on linen,
25.7×36.8
Hunterian Art Gallery,
University of Glasgow

water.' At the auction 'a band of Scottish dealers fought for the Crawhall drawings . . . Thus Messrs. J. B. Bennett and Sons, of Glasgow, made the heroic bid of 1,159 gns mentioned, also giving 380 gns for a superb drawing of a cock pheasant . . . and Messrs Reid and Lefevre took, at 320 gns, the series of illustrations to "Reynarde ye Fox", exhibited at the International Society's exhibition, 1906.' He records the prices of the works by Bonington and Corot that were sold but concludes 'the day was Joe Crawhall's.' Through Reid and Lefevre, William Burrell acquired from this sale the set of ten Reynard drawings for £336 and through J. B. Bennett *Two Rabbits* (pl 77) for £57 15s.

If few records survive to document the history of these collections even less remains of the business records of William Bell Paterson (1859–1952). The fourth son of Andrew Paterson (1819–1901) a prosperous textile manufacturer, W. B. Paterson was a brother of the artist James Paterson (1854–1932) and of the architect Alexander Nisbet Paterson (1862–1947). W. B. Paterson established himself in business as a dealer with Grosvenor Thomas as Messrs Thomas and Paterson in Glasgow by 1888. That he had an early interest in the work of Crawhall is attested to by the fact that *The Aviary* was first shown at their gallery in 1888 and was then lent by Paterson to the RSW in 1889. He is listed in the Glasgow Directory for 1895–6 as 'Paterson, Wm. B. dealer in works of art, 33 Renfield St.' Around the turn of the century he opened a gallery in London at 5 Old Bond Street and his first summer exhibition, of British paintings of the eighteenth century, opened there in June 1900. Like Reid, Paterson specialised in French and Dutch paintings and in contemporary British drawings and watercolours.

If Paterson tried to specialise in the sale of Crawhall's work prior to 1900 then he was not successful. At some time, however, in the first years of the new century it was he, not Reid, who had works by the artist on display. In a letter to Mary Auras of *c*.1903, Crawhall writes 'There are two new pictures of mine at Paterson's, one not bad and one rotten.'[50] Paterson's exhibition catalogues for the period 1905 to 1908 show that the dealer had numerous works by the artist on show and it was he who in 1907 exhibited and sold the facsimiles of the Reynard series. In 1912 he organised a loan exhibition of fifty of Crawhall's most important works and in the 1920s and 1930s works by the artist were still passing through his gallery. It was he, not Reid, who was entrusted with the 1927 Coats exhibition and sale and it was to him that Burrell now turned for help to enlarge his collection of Crawhall's work.

The 1912 exhibition, accompanied by an illustrated catalogue, was important for bringing together in the last year of the artist's life much of his best work. The critic of *The Times* reviewed the exhibition at some length: 'This artist, who lives far from London and only now and then sends a drawing to a gallery for the public to see, has at last been induced to allow a loan collection of his work to be shown by Mr W. B. Paterson, 5, Old Bond Street. At first sight they might pass for rapid sketches of birds and animals, of hawks and jackdaws, poultry and ducks, horses

EXHIBITIONS, COLLECTORS AND DEALERS   101

and riders. Really they are the fruit of the most exact and careful study; moreover, they are not the result, as might be imagined, of long familiarity with Japanese prints and Chinese paintings. Many of them were done, we believe, before Mr Crawhall had seen any Oriental graphic art at all. The likeness between them and the works of Far eastern artists is to be accounted for by a similarity of method – that of long, quiet observation, the drawings being afterwards made from memory. Mr Crawhall is as yet known only to a few collectors, who are almost fanatical in their admiration of his drawings. We trust that this little exhibition will introduce a wider circle to a very interesting artist.'[51]

77
Two Rabbits
c.1893
Watercolour heightened with
bodycolour on paper,
29.5×38.0
The Burrell Collection

78
White Hen and Chickens
c.1901
Chalk, pencil and
watercolour on paper,
7.3×7.3
The Burrell Collection

5

HUMORIST AND ILLUSTRATOR

A review of Crawhall's work without consideration of his frankly
humorous drawings would be incomplete. Taciturn as he was
socially, he was ever on the alert for the funny side of life.

Adrian Bury, *Joseph Crawhall*[1]

Crawhall's unique powers of observation, skill in draughtsmanship and ready wit amply provided him with the qualifications required of the professional illustrator. While more than willing to dash off humorous, sometimes caustic, drawings for his nieces or artist friends, Crawhall was not prepared to submit to the necessary routine, the near servitude, of supplying weekly drawings to an illustrated journal. With no wife or family to support and with a private income, he could afford to work when the mood came upon him. There is no doubt that, because of this, the surviving sketches and illustrations are of a consistently high quality.

While many of these personal mementoes have remained with the families of those for whom they were originally executed, a number have found their way into a public collection. In 1922 Sir William Burrell purchased forty-six works from Mrs Black-Hawkins for the sum of £800. Most of the letters, drawings and watercolours purchased had been executed by Crawhall for Mary Auras – the maiden name of Mrs Black-Hawkins.

As has been discussed in a previous chapter Crawhall would have met Mary through John Lavery. Although some writers have hinted at a romantic attachment between the young model and Crawhall, it seems much more likely that the relationship was a platonic one, based on a shared sense of humour and a love of animals. Mary must have found communication in English difficult, and her

79
Owl and Bees
c.1903
Gouache on linen,
26.5×35.8
The Burrell Collection

innocence and possible vulnerability would have appealed to the protective side of
Crawhall's nature. The letter illustrated with *Lady Riding a Camel* (pl 57) seems
to confirm this interpretation of the relationship. Crawhall writes, '[Mary] you
could never have had such a good time in all your short life as you are having now.
When you come back you must tell me all about it. I have not forgotten your Ex
Libris but I have not done it yet, all in good time. My love to Eileen and John,
Yours very sincerely, J. Crawhall.'

The drawings are largely humorous observations – of life in Morocco, or of his
beloved animal subjects. Many bear the inscription 'To Mary Auras' (pl 79) or
sometimes, simply 'M.A.' (pl 78). While many are obviously hasty sketches on
scrap paper, others are valuable studies executed in gouache on linen. In *Owl and
Bees* (pl 79), under a moonlit sky and set against the vaguest indication of a town –
where darkened buildings are relieved by squares of light – we witness the evident
consternation and puzzlement of an owl being accosted by a swarm of bees. As is
typical of Crawhall's later work, it is the linen itself that provides the warm
background colour. The soft, round shape of the owl is wittily contrasted with the
jagged and threatening wings and legs of the bees, a contrast that is continued in
the play of vibrant orange on the bees against the comfortable brown tones of the
owl.

Highlander Playing the Bagpipes (pl 80) could well be a humorous comment on
both his father's taste in music and his mother's nationality. Unlike *Owl and Bees*
this wash drawing would have been executed in a matter of minutes. From a

number of surviving letters it is clear that Crawhall kept in contact with Mary as she travelled in Europe and North Africa with Lavery and Eileen. These letters are usually illustrated and must have been a joy to receive. *Butterfly Lady in Switzerland* (pl 81) illustrates a letter written from Crawhall's home at Brandsby,

80
Highlander Playing the Bagpipes
1900
Wash on paper, 37.8×24.9
The Burrell Collection

81
Butterfly Lady in Switzerland
c.1902
Ink and wash on paper,
15.2×10.0
The Burrell Collection

82
Fox Terrier and Puppies
c.1891
Ink and wash on paper,
12.7×17.8
The Burrell Collection

83
Foxhound and Puppies
c.1903
Gouache on linen,
13.5×17.5
The Burrell Collection

84
Irresistible Force: Immovable
Object
c.1890
Watercolour on paper,
14.3×22.2

near Easingwold in Yorkshire. Crawhall writes, 'My dear Mary, I am glad to learn that you are enjoying Zurich it must be jolly to be able to amuse oneself in snow and ice. I am afraid it would kill me dead . . . Do you do this sort of thing?' The sketch is Crawhall's humorous and imaginative rendering of a Swiss mountain village. Tiny locals hike their way up a mountain, while a bemused cow chews the cud in the foreground. Dominating the sky, a sylph-like lady, unsuitably clad in stylish hat and a full-length gown and balanced on lengthy bits of wood as if on skis, glides gracefully down, no doubt on account of her wings. As in *Owl and Bees* it is the material – here the blue writing paper – that provides the background colour, with touches of blue, green and yellow resulting in a jewel-like whole.

While reticent in the company of adults, Crawhall was, according to the testimony of his contemporaries, fond of children. One of his nieces described how they 'all loved Uncle Lossie. He was very gentle and quiet, and did not talk much but sometimes when we sat a little later than usual he would tell us about his adventures in Morocco. He was not a joyous man, rather sad and very delicate and we were never allowed to disturb him when he was painting. He explained to me once that his painting was a gift and that if he was disturbed the inspiration was gone. He cared nothing for worldly honour, and hated snobbery . . . He would always draw and paint and amuse us children. We would watch him as with lightning strokes of the brush, in two or three minutes, he made a lovely picture for us. Sometimes for fun he would only reveal what he was painting in the last few strokes. He used our brushes and paints and our penny drawing-books, but we never went into his studio. A cousin told me that she told him once that she had never seen any of his pictures, and that she found later that he had brought a picture down and arranged it for her to see. It was so lovely that she could not speak, and he, perhaps interpreting her silence wrongly, must have destroyed it, for it was never seen again.'[2]

The subject-matter and the simplicity of treatment of *Fox Terrier and Puppies* (pl 82) and *Foxhound and Puppies* (pl 83) make one feel these must have been drawn for a young child. Yet the artistry, though concealed, is striking. In *Foxhound and Puppies* only a few lines conjure up the outline and fullness of form of the row of dogs staring intently into the fire. Strokes of orange highlight and follow the curves of the seated puppies, contrasting with the lines of the gate. *Irresistible Force: Immovable Object* (pl 84), while humorous, probably has a more serious purpose. The 'R.W.' branded on one of the sheep is an abbreviation for Crawhall's brother-in-law, Richard Walton. Walton, it seems, did not always see eye to eye with other members of the family. *Study of Mice* (pl 85) once belonged to one of Walton's daughters. It is related to Crawhall's jokey end-piece for his father's book *Border Notes* – where two mice are watching as another, indicated only by his tail, disappears into a trap. Many similar drawings were originally in the collection of Richard Walton, including *The Rabbits* (pl 86). Crawhall, as usual, at the expense of man, sides with the animals. In *The Rabbits*

85
Study of Mice
c.1890
Watercolour on paper,
14.0×22.5
Private Collection

he has deliberately rubbed away an area of black on the rabbits to give the effect of light shining on the fur – a technique he often used.

Crawhall would certainly have designed family greetings cards and a humorous example – probably sent to E. A. Walton – is the *New Year Greeting*, 1884 (pl 87), of a bird-pallette greeting a cat-paint tube. A competent artist in black and white, Crawhall could have earned a living as an illustrator. Charles Keene may well have tried to encourage him in this direction as is suggested in a letter discussing an impending visit to the Crawhalls to attend a bagpipe competition in 1879. Keene mentions that he had told *The Graphic* that the competition would be a good subject: 'A sketch might suit them. Your son might have a shy with a sketch of a piper and his pipes.'[3]

Another contemporary who could have influenced Crawhall in this respect was Phil May (1864–1903). May's work for *Punch*, *The Graphic* and the *Illustrated London News* amongst others was admired for its humanity and humour and for his ability to embrace both ends of the social order. Admired by Whistler, May, like Crawhall but unlike most of his contemporaries, eliminated as much line as possible thereby achieving the same appearance of spontaneity. Both artists aimed to simplify and reduce, May stating that when he could use fewer lines in a drawing, he would expect double the salary!

May's output, however, was prolific for, unlike Crawhall, he had a wife to support and also loved to entertain, which was expensive. Both artists shared a love of horses and according to contemporaries there was a marked physical resemblance between the two men.[4] May's biographer commented that 'Phil May liked to build up his image as a travelled man, which went well with his carefully contrived sporty appearance, his check coats, well-cut breeches and shining leather gaiters. A contemporary with much the same taste in dress . . . was the animal painter Joseph Crawhall. . . . Crawhall and May had a high opinion of each other's work, though their first meeting at the Savage Club had been engineered by Raven-Hill for a different reason: they so closely resembled one another in appearance. When they met, each stared at the other in speechless amazement.'[5]

If Crawhall was not to respond to the influence of Keene and May, he was prepared to collaborate in the illustration of a number of his father's books. The publication in 1880 of his father's *Border Notes and Mixty-Maxty* marked Crawhall junior's début as an illustrator. He was to contribute to many publications, including *Chap-book Chaplets* (1883), *Chorographia or A Survey of Newcastle upon Tyne* (1884), *Old Aunt Elspa's Spelling* (1884/5), *Izaak Walton: His Wallet Booke* (1885) and *Impresses Quaint* (1889). However it was his father who actually cut or engraved all the illustrations.

Crawhall's most substantial contributions are to be found in Crawhall senior's *The Compleatest Angling Book that euer was writ* (1881) and *Old ffrendes wyth newe Faces* (1883). Here, the son's superior drawing skills and love of animals are complemented and contrasted with Crawhall senior's crude cuts and his interest in the delineation of human character. The original edition of *The Compleatest Angling Booke* was anonymous and contained illustrations by various members of the Crawhall family. In the second edition the major change is in the pictorial

87
New Year Greeting
1884
Ink on paper, 9.1×11.2
National Gallery of Scotland,
Edinburgh

86
The Rabbits
c.1890
Watercolour and pencil on
paper, 16.5×23.5
Private Collection

88

88–91
Illustration from Joseph Crawhall's Compleatest Angling
Booke, *2nd ed. 1881 by Joseph Crawhall junior (88), James
Guthrie (89, 90) and by both together (91)*

89

90

Wood's the thing after all

91

content with ink sketches by Crawhall junior and James Guthrie replacing some of the prints by Crawhall senior's brothers and sisters. The resulting book is very much lighter in tone but one criticism that has been levied against this edition is the lack of relationship between illustrations and text. Crawhall junior also contributed the Preface tail-piece, and a humorous drawing of a bull chasing an angler, with mud and fish flying (pl 88).

Various depictions of anglers, ranging in style from bold sketches akin to Crawhall's bull, to sardonic idylls (pl 89) mark Guthrie's contribution. *Wood's the Thing After All* (pl 91) is a joint work – Guthrie providing the figures and, appropriately, Crawhall junior the dog. Guthrie's etching of Crawhall senior (pl 90) humorously captures an elderly, care-worn angler, complete with beard. Guthrie's biographer Caw wrote that these sketches 'are marked by a special verve of drawing, a very spirited use of black and white, and a boisterous and sardonic vein of humour.'[6]

Olde ffrendes wyth newe Faces (Adorn'd with futable SCULPTURES), 1883, contains a number of coloured sketches by Crawhall junior. Unlike the illustrations to *The Compleatest Angling Booke* these are related to the text. The rearing horse (pl 92) has a demonic feel wholly appropriate to the story it illustrates. The

92
An illustration by Joseph Crawhall in his father's Olde ffrendes wyth newe Faces, *1883*

93
An illustration by Joseph Crawhall inhis father's Olde ffrendes wyth new Faces, *1883*

94
Red Deer in the Coto
Doñana, Spain
1890
Wash heightened with
bodycolour on brown paper,
28.0×21.0
Private Collection

tale of a murder ends with a group of men appearing on horseback at the dead of night. Crawhall's drawing shows the moment when the first shot is fired. By contrast, the ink and wash sketch of sheep on a hillside (pl 93) is pastoral and tranquil. The composition, with its emphasis on design rather than detail, is close to many paintings of the same period by others of the Glasgow Boys.

A number of Crawhall's drawings were included in a book by his cousin, Abel Chapman (1851–1929). Chapman, an amateur bird and animal painter, was the son of a brewery owner. Business entailed travel and Chapman took the opportunity to pursue his interest in hunting and natural history, making expeditions which eventually were to take him throughout Europe and into North, South and East Africa. He was the first to suggest a game reserve in the Eastern Transvaal, the Sabi Sanctuary, now known as Kruger National Park. His many books describe his experiences and are often illustrated with his own drawings. Today many of his drawings, big game trophies and natural history specimens form part of the collection of the Hancock Museum in Newcastle.

Crawhall senior leaves us a valuable record of the relationship between the two families. In a letter to his sister Mary, of 1889, he writes, 'Abel's book has given me great pleasure – it's a right good book well and logically written by an educated master of language.' A few weeks later he writes again, confessing to have been very confused trying to talk to Abel about birds. 'I tried hard to talk bird and while I was discussing Flamingo that minx Ethel came smiling into the room . . . I got so mixed I believe I confounded the subject matter of discourse with Pelicans – however – there's one blessing – Abel would see I knew nothing of what I was talking about . . .' The letter continues with him confessing to having had a similar problem when discussing electricity with Professor Garrett, '. . . my wife frowned like a door knocker . . . I'm afraid I was found out there too.'[7]

In 1910 Chapman's *Unexplored Spain* was published. Containing two hundred and nine illustrations, it included works by Joseph Crawhall, E. Caldwell and Abel Chapman. The author explained that, as he felt the camera does not always catch the right image, he had used illustrations rather than photographs, where possible. The book is devoted to the wildlife of Spain and he is careful to explain that the 'Spain that we love and of which we write is not the Spain of tourist or globe-trotter.'[8] The third chapter describes the Coto Doñana, a sand-barrier forming forty miles of Spanish coastline, whose maximum breadth is ten miles. Centuries ago this had been the hunting ground of the Dukes of Medina Sidonia and of the Spanish kings from the time of Philip IV. The chief game of the area was red deer and wild boar. He goes on to describe it as a place of sand and sand-dunes, a 'singular exotic patch of African desert . . . tacked on to the southernmost confines of Europe.'[9] The following chapter includes Crawhall's *Red Deer in the Coto Doñana* (pl 94), one of six drawings illustrating the life of the deer. Three bullfight subjects are also included in a chapter that traces the origins and developments of the Spanish tradition. Chapman reused Crawhall's illustrations in his later autobiographical *Retrospect: Reminiscences 1851–1928*.

Illustrations by Crawhall were to appear in many other publications, including *The Yellow Book*, and in articles by his friends George Denholm Armour and the Duke of Frias. One has the distinct feeling, however, that with the exception of the illustrations to *Olde ffrendes* these drawings existed quite independently of the publications, for only once is Crawhall known to have accepted an official commission.

This commission in 1896 by Thomas Glen Arthur was for a series of ten illustrations which he intended to bind into a copy of the fables of Reynard the Fox. When Arthur relinquished this idea the drawings were sold to the dealer W. B. Paterson who later sold them to W. A. Coats. It was Coats who gave permission for the drawings to be reproduced in facsimile and offered to the public in 1906 at ten guineas in a limited edition of two hundred copies. Sir William Burrell acquired all ten originals through Alexander Reid from the Coats sale at Christie's on 12 April 1935. Executed at Brockenhurst, Hampshire, *c*.1896–7, this series gave Crawhall the chance of distilling the essence of many years of observing animal life.[10]

Brockenhurst was the home of one of Crawhall's sisters and it is likely that Crawhall and his mother went to stay there in the period immediately following Crawhall senior's death. It is equally possible, that, as a result of a period of financial uncertainty, he was prepared to accept this commission.

Reynard the Fox is the central figure of the medieval French collection of stories (grouped under the title of the *Roman de Renart*) and of later works of a similar nature, in which the characters are not humans but animals. There were narrative poems about Reynard in English, French, Flemish, German and Italian extant in the Middle Ages. A Latin version is dated about 1150 and an early French version *c*.1175. In these Reynard is the villainous hero of an animal epic. While the early versions are lighthearted, later versions give way to more moralising allegory. In these Reynard becomes the personification of hypocrisy, deceit and evil – a symbol of sin, the Devil in disguise.

The escapades of the fox and the unscrupulous tricks he plays on other inhabitants of the animal kingdom are related with each animal designated by name and having its own individual character. The aim was primarily to amuse and the stories had immediate and widespread popularity. The humour is simple and direct, and often bawdy. Elements of animal realism are combined with human characterisation. Crawhall's willingness to fulfil the commission must also have been because of his empathy with the subject. His drawings appear to illustrate the late medieval Dutch prose version (Middle Dutch *Die hystorie van Reynaert die Vos* of 1479) translated into English by William Caxton in 1481 as *The History of Reynard the Fox* (reprinted 1489). Caxton not only printed the book but was also editor and translator.

Reynard is the archetypal folk-hero who 'in no way represents the little man, even though he is a protagonist of average proportions. He would be inappropriate as a sociological or political symbol, despite the fact that his first and last impulse is to survive and that he consistently portrays the innocently oppressed and only on occasion the oppressor. He is human enough to possess a streak of genuine meanness, a degree of unpredictability, and a devastating flair for fake humility.'[11] Reynard has been described as 'chiefly a rather good-natured criticism of the human race in general.'

Crawhall's illustrations sometimes coincide in subject-matter with the subjects

95
*Curtois, the Hound, at
Noble's Court*
c.1896
*Watercolour on paper,
25.3×31.0*
The Burrell Collection

treated by the woodcut master known as the Haarlem Master who flourished in the 1470s in Haarlem in the Netherlands. This cycle of Reynardian woodcuts was imitated right into the nineteenth century, but especially by Wynkyn De Worde at the beginning of the fifteenth century. Crawhall's treatment of the subjects are, however, always original.[12]

Before the history proper, the reader is addressed by the author and informed that much learning is contained within the book 'by which points men may learn to come to the subtle knowledge of such things as daily be used . . .' and that it is 'made for need and profit of all good folk . . .' so they can see the 'subtle deceits that daily be used in the world, not to the intent that men should use them, but that every man should eschew and keep him from the subtle false shrews that they be not deceived.' In other words the book must be read and re-read '. . . for a man shall not with once over reading find the right understanding nor comprise it well.'[13] This is an important point because Crawhall also successfully veils the meaning in his illustrations – all is not revealed at the first glance.

The scene at Noble's court is the traditional opening illustration in the ancient woodcut cycle. About the time of Pentecost or Whitsuntide 'the noble king' held an open court and all beasts were commanded to attend. All came 'save Reynard the fox, for he knew himself faulty and guilty in many things against many beasts that thither should come that he dared not adventure to go thither when the king of all beasts had assembled all his court.'[14] One of the complainants is Curtois, 'a little hound . . . and complained to the king how that in the cold winter in the hard frost, he had been sore forwintered in such wise as he had kept no more meat than a pudding, which pudding Reynard the fox had taken away from him.'[15] It is this scene that is depicted in *Curtois, the Hound, at Noble's Court* (pl 95). Crawhall, using artistic licence, embroiders on the original by including elephants, camels

96
*Chanticleer and the Funeral
Procession of Coppen
c.1896
Watercolour on paper,
25.2×31.5
The Burrell Collection*

and flamingoes, and by portraying Noble, the lion, with a bottle between his paws.
The viewer is sited in this audience directly behind the bear — by implication,
therefore, we are present at the scene.

In *Chanticleer and the Funeral Procession of Coppen* (pl 96) Crawhall keeps
more rigorously to the printed word. Just as Grimbert, one of Reynard's relations,
is justifying the fox's behaviour '. . . so saw they come down the hill to them
Chanticleer the cock, and brought on a bier a dead hen, of whom Reynard had
bitten the head off and that must be showed to the king for to have knowledge
thereof.' 'Chanticleer came forth and smote piteously his hands and his feathers;
and on each side of the bier went two sorrowful hens. That one was called Cantart
and that other good hen Crayant. They were two the fairest hens that were
between Holland and Ardennes. These hens bore each of them a burning taper,
which was long and straight. These two hens were Coppen's sisters and they cried
so piteously "Alas and well away" for the death of their dear sister Coppen. Two
young hens bore the bier, which cackled so heavily and wept so loud for the death
of Coppen, their mother, that it was far heard. Thus came they together tofore the
king.'[16] Coppen, one of Chanticleer's daughters, was the eleventh of his fifteen
children to have been killed by Reynard.

Crawhall selects the moment when the funeral procession has reached the top of
the hill, delighting in portraying the confusion of feathers, blood and tears and
quite intentionally forcing the viewer to work his way slowly through the
procession. It is only after some time that the reason for the mourning, the dead
hen, is discerned. Throughout the series Crawhall varies the format of the
illustrations between landscape and portrait, depending on the appropriateness
for the subject in hand.

Even more difficult to discern is the situation in *How Bruin, the Bear, Ate the Honey* (pl 97). Having taken counsel as to how to punish Reynard, Noble asks Bruin to bring Reynard to the court. Bruin is warned by the king of Reynard's cunning. He '. . . knows so many wiles that he shall lie and flatter and shall think how he may beguile, deceive, and bring you to some mockery.'[17]

Bruin travels through the forest to Reynard's home at Maleperduys. Reynard greets the bear and, seemingly concerned for Bruin's well-being, points out that he would have attended court the following day without having been summoned. Reynard is 'too full' to travel because he has 'eaten so much new meat'. Reynard pretends to have been eating honey. Bruin falls right into the fox's trap: 'Lief Reynard, help me that I might get a deal of this honey and as long as I live, I shall be to you a true friend and abide by you as far as you help me that I may have a part of this honey.'[18]

Reynard informs him that the honey belongs to a husbandman Lantfert and that Bruin can have as much as he wants, as long as he promises to help Reynard against his enemies at court. They make their way into Lantfert's yard. Lantfert, 'a strong carpenter of great timber . . . had brought that other day tofore into his yard a great oak which he had begun to cleave. And as men be wont, he had smitten two betels therein one after that other, in such wise the oak was wide open. . . .' Reynard tells Bruin that the honey is in the tree. 'Bruin the bear hastened sore toward the honey and tread in with his two foremost feet and put his head over his ears into the cleft. And Reynard sprang lightly and broke out the

97
How Bruin, the Bear, Ate the Honey
c.1896
Watercolour on paper,
24.0×31.8
The Burrell Collection

98
*Tibert, the Cat, Caught in the
Grin*
c.1896
Watercolour on paper,
31.0×22.9
The Burrell Collection

99
Cock Escaping from Reynard
c.1896
Watercolour on paper,
30.2×24.6
The Burrell Collection

100
*Isegrim, the Wolf, and the
Mare*
c.1896
Watercolour on paper,
30.8×24.1
The Burrell Collection

101
*Bellin the Ram, Cuwart the
Hare and Reynard the Fox*
c.1896
Watercolour on paper,
31.0×21.2
The Burrell Collection

betel of the tree.' 'Tho helped the bear neither flattery nor chiding. He was fast shut in the tree.'[19]

Bruin's howls bring Lantfert and his neighbours out into the yard, and it is only after great effort and with serious injury that Bruin eventually escapes. Again Crawhall has chosen his moment well. The composition with its strong diagonal and the foliage masking Reynard is reminiscent of a Japanese print.

Tibert, the Cat, Caught in the Grin (pl 98) illustrates the fate of the next unfortunate sent to bring Reynard to court. Tibert does not want to go: '. . . they that this counselled you were not my friends. What shall I do there? He will not for me neither come nor abide . . . I am little and feeble.' Tibert is told, however, that he 'be wise and well learned. Though you be not great, there lies not on; many do more with craft and cunning than with might and strength.'[20]

Tibert like Bruin is also attracted by the promise of food, though not honey. 'If you gave me a good fat mouse, I should be better pleased.'[21] The scene takes place by moonlight and Crawhall suggests the darkness of night. Enticed by Reynard's suggestion of mice to the priest's barn, having first sworn his allegiance to the fox, Tibert enters by a hole in the wall. Unbeknownst to him, the priest, angered by Reynard who had stolen a hen the previous night, has set a grin. Tibert is a bit nervous – he knows priests are wily and shrewish – but Reynard is scathing: 'Oho, Tibert,' says the fox, 'I saw you never so sore afraid. What ails you?' 'The cat was ashamed and sprang into the hole. And anon he was caught in the grin by the neck ere he wist.'[22] The terrified Tibert springs up and is almost strangled.

Cock Escaping from Reynard (pl 99) could be one of two scenes. Reynard is eventually persuaded to come to court by Grimbert. On the journey Reynard confesses to many of his crimes. Grimbert suggests that Reynard read his psalms, attend church, fast, keep holy days, give alms and leave his sinful life behind. The fox has only just promised to do so when 'A little beside the way as they went stood a cloister of black nuns, where many geese, hens, and capons went without the walls. And as they went talking, the fox brought Grimbert out of the right way thither; and without the walls by the barn went the poultry. The fox espied them and saw a fat young capon which went along from his fellows and lept and caught him that the feathers flew around his ears. But the capon escaped.'[23] Close in format to Tibert, both works depict an animal leaping off the ground, fur or feathers flying, in pain or anguish and in fear of its life.

On the other hand there is a later incident that this scene might possibly be intended to represent. This takes place after the scene of the pilgrimage when the coney Lampreel is attacked by Reynard, who is passing in the guise of a pilgrim. 'I saluted him but he spoke not one word, but he raught out his right foot and dubbed me in the neck between my ears that I had weened I should have lost my head. . . . I was so light that I sprang from him. . . . Though I escaped from him, I lost my one ear and I had four great holes in my head of his sharp nails that the blood sprang out and that I was nigh all aswoon.'[24]

102
*Corbant, the Rook, and
Reynard*
c.1896
*Watercolour on paper,
24.0×30.5*
The Burrell Collection

Reynard is eventually brought to court and narrowly escapes the gallows by
promising the king and queen buried treasure – greed once more. In *Bellin the
Ram, Cuwart the Hare and Reynard the Fox* (pl 101) we see Reynard setting out
on a pilgrimage, made necessary he claims, for he is under the Pope's ban and
sentence. Bellin the ram is brought to bless Reynard's mail and staff and then,
with Cuwart, is asked to accompany Reynard on the first few hundred yards of his
journey. 'And if you had seen Reynard, how personally he went with his mail and
plaster on his shoulder, and the shoes on his feet, you should have laughed. He
went and showed him outward wisely, but he laughed in his heart.'[25] Crawhall
manages to suggest the menace behind Reynard's disguise and delights in the
details of the vestments. Cuwart is soon dead.

In terms of legibility, the most difficult of the series to decipher is *Corbant, the
Rook, and Reynard* (pl 102). The feasting at court is interrupted by Corbant the
rook. 'Dear Lord, hear me! I bring you here a piteous complaint. I went today by
the morrow with Sharpbeak, my wife, for to play upon the heath and there lay
Reynard the fox down on the ground like a dead caitiff. His eyes stared and his
tongue hung long out of his mouth like a hound had been dead. We tasted and felt
his belly, but we found thereon no life. Tho went my wife and harkened and laid
her ear tofore his mouth for to wit if he drew his breath, which misfell her evil. For
the false fell fox awaited well his time and when he saw her so nigh him, he caught
her by the head and bit it off.' Corbant escaped to the safety of a nearby tree but
then was an unwilling witness as 'the false caitiff ate and slonked her in so hungrily
that he left neither flesh nor bone, no more but a few feathers.'[26]

Crawhall only provides the slightest clue as to the situation here, for Reynard, other than his brush, is well hidden. Using the same washes that have enlivened all of these illustrations, he shows his skill in bringing life to the variety of blacks – a rich blue in the feathers of the rook contrasting with the warm browns of Reynard's fur.

It might seem fantasy that a fox should pretend to be dead in this way, but it has been pointed out that a fox simulating death to capture unwary birds is, indeed, true and based on observation. Perhaps Crawhall himself, in his long hours observing animals in their natural habitat, witnessed such a scene.[27]

One of the most sparkling of the series, and appropriately so, is Crawhall's illustration of *Isegrim, the Wolf, and the Mare* (pl 100). Setting off once more for the court, Reynard again confesses to Grimbert. He tells first of his more recent sins and then says, 'I have forgotten one thing the last time that I was shriven to you, which I have sith bethought me and it was a great deceit that I did which I now will tell you.

'I came with the wolf walking between Houthulst and Elverding. There saw we go a red mare and she had a black colt or a foal of four months old, which was good and fat. Isegrim was almost starved for hunger and prayed me go to the mare and wit of her if she would sell her foal. I ran fast to the mare and asked that of her. She said she would sell it for money. I demanded to her how she would sell it. She said, "It is written on my hinder foot. If you can read and be a clerk, you may come and read it." Tho wist I well where she would be and I said, "Nay, forsooth I cannot read and also I desire not to buy your child. Isegrim has sent me hither and would fain know the price thereof." The mare said, "Let him come then himself and I shall let him have knowledge." ' Reynard then confesses to Isegrim that as he never went to school, he is unable to read and so Isegrim must read for him. Isegrim boasts of how he can read French, Latin, English and Dutch. When Isegrim asks to read off of the mare's hoof, 'She said "Do" and lifted up her foot, which was new shod with iron and six strong nails and she smote him without missing on his head that he fell down as he had been dead. A man should well have ridden a mile ere he arose. The mare trotted away with her colt and she left Isegrim lying shrewdly hurt and wounded. He lay and bled and howled as a hound.'[28]

Another flashback scene is captured in *Reynard, the Fox, and Isegrim's Wife* (pl 103) although on this occasion it is Isegrim who tells the court the sad tale. 'This false thief betrayed my wife once, foul and dishonestly. It was so that in a winter's day that they went together through a great water and he bore my wife on hand that he would teach her to take fish with her tail and that she should let it hang in the water a good while and there should so much fish cleave on it that four of them should not con eat it. The fool my wife supposed he had said truth and she went in the mire to the belly too, ere she came into the water. And when she was in the deepest water, he bade her hold her tail till that the fish were come. She held her tail so long that it was frozen hard in the ice and could not pluck it out. And when he saw that he sprang up after on her body. Alas there ravished he and forced my

103
Reynard, the Fox, and
Isegrim's Wife
c.1896
Watercolour on paper,
30.6×24.5
The Burrell Collection

104
Dame Rukenaw the She-Ape
Counsels Reynard
c.1896
Watercolour on paper,
30.4×22.0
The Burrell Collection

wife so knavishly that I am ashamed to tell it. She could not defend herself, the silly beast, she stood so deep in the mire. Hereof he cannot say nay, for I found him with the deed. For as I went above upon the bank, I saw him beneath upon my wife shouting and sticking as men do when they do such work and play. Alas, what pain suffered I tho at my heart. I had almost for sorrow lost my five wits and cried as loud as I might "Reynard, what do you there!" And when he saw me so nigh, tho leapt he off and went his way.'[29]

Not part of the traditional woodcut series, this illustration again requires patient interpretation. Through the falling snow we glimpse Isegrim in the woods. Tell-tale paw marks lead us to Reynard who is just disappearing off to the right, but the figure of the howling wolf does not seem to resemble that animal at all, so distorted is she by pain and her unfortunate position.

In the last scene *Dame Rukenaw the She-Ape Counsels Reynard* (pl 104) to victory in the field of battle against Isegrim. Once more this scene is not contained in the traditional woodcut cycle. The fox, of course, survives the duel, not without utilising some underhand methods, and the tale ends with the familiar words: 'And the fox lived forthon with his wife and his children in great joy and gladness.'[30] Deserving to be better known, this series is proof that, had Crawhall been so inclined, he could, like his father, have been a celebrated illustrator.

CHAPTER

6

A LOVE OF ANIMALS

In a few lines he could sketch an animal, making it more
recognisable than the most candid camera could do – and this
from memory. If he did a pack of hounds the huntsman would be
able to recognise every single one, even when it was indicated in
half a dozen marks on the linen or paper he happened to be
working on.

John Lavery, *The Life of a Painter*[1]

Unlike many Victorian artists who pandered to the popular taste for a sentimental depiction of animals, Crawhall, as his sister Elspeth noted, 'loved animals and would not use them for base purposes for he respected their individuality too much.'[2] Many of Crawhall's contemporaries commented on the fact that the artist was more at ease with the animals he loved and understood than with human beings. With just a few strokes of his brush he could capture an animal's character and personality and these 'seeming sketches contain more truth beautifully expressed than is to be found in the most finished Landseer.'[3] Reviewing the 1894 Crawhall exhibition Frank Rinder stated that, in his opinion, Crawhall's 'Black Rabbit may well be the nineteenth century equivalent of Dürer's wonderful Hare.'[4] Crawhall's depictions of animals tend to be revelations rather than factual records, for just as he was not interested in pursuing illustration as a profession, he had no desire to earn his living as a portraitist of horses, their riders or of family pets.

The Aviary (pl 106), exhibited extensively at home and abroad in 1889 and 1890, established Crawhall's reputation as a watercolourist. Crawhall had visited Clifton Zoo in Bristol in 1888 and the central building in the Zoo's gardens was

PARROT HOUSE, CLIFTON ZOOLOGICAL GARDENS, BRISTOL (NO. 1505).

105
Anonymous
Parrot House, Clifton
Zoological Gardens, Bristol
c.1910
Postcard

the so-called 'Parrot House'. There coloured macaws, gaudy Amazon parrots, dull-toned African parrots and parrakeets could be seen perched on poles feeding or flying up to startle the unwary visitor. The Zoo's annual reports record many gifts of birds in this period. One Revd Matthews donated 'twenty-four valuable parrots' in 1885 and in 1886 gave 'two red-crested cockatoos, three lemon-crested cockatoos, one Roselle Parrakeet, one Leadbieter Parrakeet, two King Parrots, two White-Fronted Amazons, four Delectas, two pairs of Amazons and two monkeys.' This generosity might well have been associated with the decision, recorded in the Zoo's *Fiftieth Annual Report* of April 1886, to set aside the sum of £400 for the reconstruction of the bird house. 'Believing that the present building is past repair and that a new bird house (if properly constructed) would become one of the most attractive features of the Gardens, the Committee, after careful consideration, recommend that the amount realised by the sale of the new shares (about £400) be devoted to the purpose above alluded to, and a special resolution to that effect would be moved at the Annual Meeting.'[5]

A later report records that the 'new Bird and Reptile House is one of the best improvements made in the Gardens of late years; it is very popular, and attracts many visitors.'[6] It is this new Bird House that Crawhall has so marvellously suggested in *The Aviary*. Some idea of the original appearance of the building, closed in 1969, can be seen in an early photograph (pl 105). Although it is the parrot in the foreground of *The Aviary* that immediately captures the attention, by selecting a viewpoint slightly to the right of the centre of the room Crawhall encourages the viewer to read back into the picture space along the line of the birds' stands. Gradually the patient viewer will make out the hastily indicated wall-cages, the wooden posts of which emphasise the vertical nature of the

106
The Aviary, Clifton
1888
Watercolour on paper,
51.0×35.0
The Burrell Collection

J. Crawhall

Clifton.
'83.

picture's design. Behind the wire mesh of these cages more birds can be discerned. One of these almost looks as if it is perched on the hat of one of the two ladies in the background. The vague washes and the manner of indicating these dimly perceived birds prefigures Crawhall's later treatment of caged birds in *The Dove* (Tate Gallery, London). An early biographer records that the two women are 'Crawhall's and James Guthrie's sisters.'[7] While it is possible that one of Crawhall's sisters is portrayed, the Miss Guthrie, if indeed she is a Miss Guthrie, was more likely to have been the sister of the Headmaster of the nearby Clifton College School as Guthrie's sister had moved to New Zealand by 1888.

Crawhall was as capable of capturing birds in movement as at rest. In *The Rook's Nest* (pl 74) and *A Mallard Rising* (pl 64) he uses a more sweeping diagonal to suggest and describe the flight of the two birds. The regular pattern of coloured reflections in *A Mallard Rising* is not allowed to interfere with his careful description of the bird as it rises from the water. There is much less description in his rook which, viewed from below and presumably from some distance, is yet no less accurate in its characterisation. The darkness of the bird and the bareness of the branches are contrasted with the brilliant blue of the sky which seems to echo the bird's screech. *The Spanish Cock and Snail* (pl 107) combines all Crawhall's skill in witty observation with a calligraphic representation of the bird and its setting, reminiscent of Chinese wash drawings on silk.

Today Crawhall is admired by many wildlife artists who recognise and appreciate his break with the traditions and conventions of wildlife painting. His drawings distil the essence of the character of an animal or bird, capturing nuances of form, pattern and pose. Instead of working directly from nature, with the danger of being tempted to give too much detail, Crawhall worked from memory. Cunninghame Graham in *Writ in Sand* describes Crawhall's working practice: 'I hardly ever saw him draw direct from nature. When he had to paint a horse, a dog, a goat, or any other animal, a branch in which he excelled all painters of his time . . . he would go and look at them for a full hour, with a look so intense it seemed to burn a hole into their skin. Then perhaps, but rarely, he would take a pencil or a piece of coloured chalk out of his pocket and, on the back of an old envelope, set down cabalistic signs or dabs of colour . . . Next day, he might, or he might not, return and gaze another hour, and when one thought he had forgotten all about the animal, produce a painting so life-like . . . that it forced one to regard the animal that he had limned just as he must have seen it for ever afterwards.'[8]

Although we usually associate Crawhall with depictions of domestic animals and birds, his travels in Tangier and Spain and visits to zoos and circuses encouraged him to depict more exotic animals. It is likely that both *The Tiger* (pl 108) and *The Tigers* (Burrell Collection) were drawn from caged animals observed at a zoo or at a circus, though in both Crawhall has managed to suggest natural movements and a natural habitat. Crawhall's sense of humour is never far away and one trusts that *The Tiger* (pl 109) is an imaginary scene. At first

107
The Spanish Cock and Snail
c.1894–9
Gouache on linen,
33.3×31.2
The Burrell Collection

108
The Tiger
c.1894–1906
Gouache on linen,
32.0×49.5
Private Collection

astounded by the economy of means in the delineation of the tiger, the viewer only later notices the dismembered body of an unwary native. Great splodges of blood brighten the left foreground, contrasting with the peaceful scene of cattle grazing and the skyline of an eastern town in the background. Like so many of Crawhall's humorous drawings this was formerly in the collection of his brother-in-law Richard Walton.

Local circuses in Newcastle or Hengler's Cirque in Glasgow may have inspired Crawhall's many scenes of circus interiors. Most convey the colour and mystery of the spectacle but few have the air of sadness of *The Circus* (pl 110). Here the emphatic horizontals of the ringside fence, the balancing pole, the seated animals and the profiled horse are played off against the strong vertical accents of the clown and a distant ladder. In this way the composition itself heightens the feeling of tension as the performing dog, precariously balanced on a ball, works its way across the thin pole. Despite the notes of red of the horse's pennants and the clown's make-up, and the green, red and yellow jackets of the tiny monkeys, the overall keynote of *The Circus* is a cold greyness that suggests Crawhall intended the work as a comment on the fragility of existence, rather in the way Picasso was to do some years later in his Harlequin series.

In his childhood Crawhall had played truant from school to visit fairs and circuses, fostering a love that was to remain with him throughout his life. In the 1890s, after his family had moved to London, he was a frequent visitor to the annual fair in the London borough of Barnet. Attracted by the horses rather than the funfair, Crawhall captured the colour and atmosphere of this centuries-old event in *Barnet Fair* (pl 111). Barnet has had an official market since 1199 when King John gave a charter to the abbot and monks of St Albans permitting a market 'in the village of Barnet on one day in the week, to wit, Thursday. . . .'[9] In 1588 Queen Elizabeth I granted a charter to the Lord of the Manor of Barnet, Charles Butler, giving him the right to hold a weekly market on Mondays and a twice-yearly fair. Unlike many such fairs, Barnet's horse and cattle fair became more famous and prosperous with time. Livestock for sale included horses, cattle, sheep, pigs and goats.

By the mid-eighteenth century horse-racing was part of Barnet Fair, the races being held on the last of the three days. The races were a part of the pleasure fair which accompanied the business of horse and cattle trading. 'There were many Welsh ponies at the fair and their drovers raced them for a saddle and bridle financed by public subscription. There would be ten or twelve runners, the riders in shirt-sleeves with handkerchiefs tied round their foreheads, some with no

109
The Tiger
c.1891–3
*Watercolour heightened with bodycolour on paper,
21.0×26.0
National Gallery of Scotland,
Edinburgh*

110
The Circus
1893
Watercolour heightened with
bodycolour on paper,
45.3×61.8
The Burrell Collection

saddle, some with no bridle. The final run up the straight to the winning post would have dealers galloping alongside, yelling encouragement.'[10] It is such a scene that is depicted in *Barnet Fair: Putting Him through His Paces*, 1896 (Paul Mellon Collection, Upperville, Virginia). Formal racing was held at Barnet until 1870 but this ceased when the railway bought the land. One writer, at the end of the last century, describes the excitement of these races: 'there was one delight of old times, itself a remnant of older times . . . Astounding to relate, it attracted its thousands, miserable sight as it was. We speak of the races. The old Barnet racecourse, for Barnet Races go back into the period of remotest antiquity indeed, occupied in the days of its glory a considerable area, and its races enjoyed no little popularity . . . on [the] field on the left side of Barnet Hill, and starting from the hollow there the races ascended the hill and obtained a tolerably long and wide course from whence they could be seen by the thousands of spectators who swarmed out of London, drawn by the sight and the betting.'[11] The hill can be seen in Crawhall's *Barnet Fair* (Private Collection), where it provides the dominant motif while the horses are relegated to the horizon line and glimpsed only in the foreground. The horse fair continued after 1870 on the fields and dales to either side of the new railway station. Today, the horse and pleasure fair are separated, but in the 1890s when Crawhall painted his *Barnet Fair* (pl 111), they were combined.

Describing the pleasure fair in 1899 Father Barnfield wrote of 'the same collection of unmeaning and outlandish shows, the same marvellous theatre, the same shooting galleries, the same Aunt Sallys, which have always been.'[12] In *Barnet Fair* Crawhall successfully suggests the scale of the fair by indicating the head and shoulders of the two horses entering from the left, seemingly part of a procession moving down towards the dale in the background where the funfair is being held. In the distance the wagons housing the sideshows are suggested with deft brushstrokes as are the advertising boards encouraging the crowds to visit the 'largest woman in the world' or to watch the boxers. It is unusual to find Crawhall working on such a large scale and interested in painting so much background detail and yet, as ever, it is only a suggestion of detail for on closer examination we realise how few strokes and touches of colour convey the impression of distant horses and crowds. The warm brown tone of the linen provides a rich background colour which is brought to life by washes of yellow and white and by touches of blue.

As Crawhall seldom dated his works and as his style is one of remarkable consistency, it is difficult to trace his artistic development. We have no record as to when he first worked on linen but it must have been about 1893. Although most of the works on linen bear Crawhall's signature not a single one is dated. Much has

111
Barnet Fair
c.1894
Gouache on linen,
36.9 × 59.5
The Burrell Collection

been written of the sheer difficulty of working in watercolour or gouache on linen, so why did Crawhall choose to work in such a difficult medium? His biographer Sutherland interviewed members of the artist's immediate family who told him that it was during a visit to Crawhall's sister in Bristol that Crawhall, finding himself without paper on which to paint, borrowed some of the brown Holland linen she used for sewing.[13] Sutherland learned more about Crawhall's technique from a professor at Reading University who had supposedly corresponded with the artist about the difficulties of painting in watercolour on linen. The linen that Crawhall used was 'light brown in colour and finally dressed in manufacture with the thinnest film of wheaten paste. So long as this film remained intact the linen presented a slightly absorbent surface very pleasant to paint on, but when once this was disturbed it would continue to absorb colour almost indefinitely. It apparently presented two possibilities; the exploitation of pure colour washes and body colour on the surface preserved intact, or the same on the surface disturbed to some extent. Crawhall, with a nice disregard for the innumerable difficulties, made use of both. Matters were further complicated by the tendency of washes to mingle unpleasantly, and by the fact, more apparent in pure watercolour, that when applied they appeared much deeper in tone than when mixed, and when dry were infinitely lighter than either.'[14]

A study of Crawhall's works on linen reveals that the artist used linen of various weights, some of it fine, as in *Cock Pheasant with Foliage and Berries* (pl 72), or relatively coarse, as in *A Mallard Rising* (pl 64). There is little evidence of Crawhall having sized or prepared the linen in any way himself, but there would have been many different finishes and sizings available and he might have experimented with a family recipe for the starching and glazing of undressed fabrics. Crawhall achieved his distinctive notes of colour by the use of Chinese White, and as in his watercolours, he frequently indicated the picture's edge by hastily washed lines of thin black. The linen could obviously not be laid on a board or mount to be worked on, as the water seeping through the linen would be retained and affect the colour washes and also distort the drying process itself. Although Sutherland states Crawhall affixed 'the cloth to a chair by four drawing pins' he could just as easily have attached it to a stretcher in the same way as one would for an oil on canvas. While it is difficult to challenge Sutherland's authority as to how Crawhall discovered the medium, it is possible that there is another explanation. Two works in the Burrell Collection, *Rabbits, Mary Auras* and *Black Spanish Cock* (pl 34) are worked on linen stretched around board. Closer examination reveals two slits in the linen, slits which would originally have held cloth straps for keeping a sketchbook closed. For both works have, in fact, been painted on the covers of one of Crawhall's sketchbooks. In these he has success-fully conquered the problem of working on linen backed by board, though both works have been executed without extensive use of water. On the whole, Crawhall's works on linen are less spontaneous than his watercolours on paper

112
*The Sportsman's Dream (on
the Eve of the 12th)*
c.1894
*Watercolour and chalk on
paper, 36.0×17.5*
Private Collection

113
Woman at Races
c.1891
*Ink and wash on paper,
36.2×23.3*
Private Collection

and probably required many more hours of work. As one writer has noted, Crawhall turned all the medium's difficulties to his advantage, being 'marvellously adroit in making the fabric suggest tone, colour and atmosphere by obliterating the grain of the fabric entirely in the light parts and allowing it to show in the dark passages or background where necessary.'[15]

Crawhall spent much of his life in amateur sporting activities and as a breeder of horses. As we have seen, it was his love of the horse that drew him to Tangier, and it was for the same reason that he went to Yorkshire where he produced some of his finest racing and hunting pictures. 'There is a certain special dignity, not recognised as it should be, about the art of him who pictures incidents of sport; it is the oldest form of the pictorial art. . . .'[16] Not all Crawhall's sporting pictures were intended as serious studies. *The Sportsman's Dream* (pl 112) represents the possible bag of a British sportsman and also includes on the top left a list of such unlikely animals as 'elephants'! There is a long popular tradition of sporting art in British painting but Crawhall, as one might expect, broke away from its accepted conventions. Crawhall's hunting pictures owe little to early sporting artists like John Wootton (*c.*1677–1765) or to nineteenth-century masters like Henry Alken Sr. (1785–1851). Crawhall's choice of subject and composition is sometimes remarkably close to that of his contemporary, Alfred Munnings (1878–1959).

114
The Race Course
c.1894–1900
Gouache on linen,
29.3×32.0
Glasgow Art Gallery and
Museum

Both artists were equally capable of capturing the distinctive stance of a horse and the appearance and movement of each and every hound in a pack. To Crawhall, however, the picture was first and foremost a work of art, and design considerations played a more important role in his hunting scenes than the recording of the events of a particular day's hunt. Similarly, Crawhall's racing scenes share nothing of the 'rocking-horse' aspect of the pictures of John Frederick Herring Sr. (1795–1865) or James Ward (1769–1859). Crawhall was arguably one of the first artists to convey accurately a galloping horse, the movements learned by careful observation rather than with the aid of a camera.

From the biographies of his friends and the testimony of his family we know that Crawhall was an assiduous attender of race-meetings throughout the country. He was even known to take his nephews and nieces with him to the races for a day's entertainment. His *Woman at Races* (pl 113) is probably a portrait of one of his sisters who, with hands deep in pockets and facing away from the jockeys, does not seem to share her brother's enthusiasm. *The Race Course* (pl 114) and *In the*

115
In the Paddock
c.1894–1900
Gouache on linen,
27.9×37.5
Private Collection

116
*Tod Sloane – The American
Jockey*
c.1899
*Watercolour on paper,
34.2×39.5*
The Burrell Collection

Paddock (pl 115) are unusual in his treatment of the theme in that, whilst concentrating on horse and rider, they suggest the social aspect of the occasion. *In the Paddock* is clearly a portrait of both horse and rider but unfortunately no documentation survives to reveal their names. This work in pose, accuracy of detail and in lighting suggests that Crawhall might have made use of photography. Once more no corroborating evidence survives. *Tod Sloane – The American Jockey* (pl 116) brilliantly captures a distinctive riding style rather than the features of either horse or jockey. Tod Sloane rode five winners at Newmarket on 30 September 1898 and a further four in April in the following year. Sloane's style was also recorded in the race pictures of Degas. It is Degas we are reminded of immediately when confronted with Crawhall's *American Jockeys* (pl 117). The emphasis on line, the use of cut-off and the asymmetry of this work all suggest the influence of the French master. It is possible that Crawhall saw some of Degas'

117
American Jockeys
c.1900
*Gouache on linen,
41.3×31.7*
Ewan Mundy Fine Art

pastels of racing scenes at an exhibition organised by Alexander Reid in his Glasgow gallery in the early 1890s.[17]

Crawhall's most exuberant treatment of the theme, *The Race* (pl 118), owes nothing to Degas but in choice of viewpoint and pose may have been influenced by Thomas Rowlandson's engraving *Dr Syntax Setting Out*.[18] With just a few strokes of black Crawhall has caught the form and volume of the racehorse's hindquarters, a feeling of muscular power emphasised by the touches of wash and bodycolour subtly suggesting the movement of the squared form. Crawhall involves us, the spectator, in the urgency and excitement of the race by using a viewpoint that implies that we too are riding a racehorse immediately following the one depicted. He uses bodycolour for the intense blue of the sky which contrasts with the pink and white of the jockey's racing silks. The impression of speed is heightened by his portrayal of the whip in motion, the Catherine wheel-like curves of white marking the passage of the whip through space. Here Crawhall is using simultaneous lines of force to suggest movement at least fifteen years before Balla and the Italian Futurists were to do so.

George Denholm Armour shared Crawhall's love of racing and hunting. In his autobiography, Denholm Armour describes their racing and hunting experiences during the years when they shared a house at Wheathampstead in Hertfordshire. Denholm Armour does not specify the years concerned but, from other written evidence, it would seem that they were together from around 1893 until 1895.[19] He describes how, after 'a couple of years at Primrose Hill studios, I decided to join with Joe Crawhall at a farmhouse in Hertfordshire, and there we stayed for two years. We ran a little joint stud and hunted with the Hertfordshire hounds, and occasionally with old Rawl's staghounds. Our experience of horse-buying in Morocco still influenced our ideas of price, and we really had some wonderful bargains. We imported from Tangier a little Barb stallion, which Crawhall had left there when he came home. Mesmuda, he was called, from the name of the place he came from [pl 119]. He was unusually small for a Barb, being only slightly over 13.2 hands high, but was all quality and a wonderful little horse.'[20] Crawhall raced Mesmuda at local 'flapper' meetings, coming in second on each of five outings, the prize money covering the days' expenses.

Denholm Armour describes the Hertfordshire countryside: 'It was all big woods and deep plough which carried little scent . . . there were few fences in the part we knew that a donkey could not have surmounted, but we enjoyed it.'[21] Their hunting experiences were translated into paint. Denholm Armour praises Crawhall 'as a great artist; I think he was the best animal painter of his time, and he did some of his finest work during the time we lived together.' He continues: 'If he did not paint many of what may be called "serious pictures", he was abundantly prolific of little humorous sketches. . . . Few people or incidents which came under his notice escaped him, but, unfortunately, he valued these things not at all, with the result that they got into all kinds of hands, and most of them have probably

118
The Race
c.1890
Watercolour heightened with bodycolour on paper,
23.2×14.2
The Burrell Collection

perished or are lost. Crawhall was a very quiet man but, when he liked, a wit. I remember one morning we met the Cockney son of our farmer landlord. The boy told Crawhall that he had shut up two ducks the night before, and found three eggs in the morning, and asked if he could explain it. "I suppose one laid the other two to one", was the prompt answer.'[22]

Denholm Armour adopted Crawhall's technique of watercolour on linen for the original studies for his book illustrations. One art historian believed that Crawhall's influence went further than this, saying that it 'was not until after he went to England . . . and came under Mr Crawhall's influence, that he developed the clear and expressive drawing which is perhaps the outstanding quality of his mature work.'[23] In countless books and in illustrated articles for *Country Life*, Denholm Armour recounted his sporting experiences, proving that the best sporting artists are also participants. Unlike Crawhall, Denholm Armour worked directly from nature. Consequently, there is always more detail and less suggestion in Denholm Armour's pictures. In his illustrations for *A Hunting Alphabet* we can see that he shared Crawhall's preference for a high horizon line and a frequent use of strong black contours but that he lacked Crawhall's assured sense of line and *mise-en-page*. Both artists shared the same sense of humour and in the works of both riders are seen falling off backwards, forwards or sideways, but in most instances with the fox escaping. Denholm Armour explained that the 'little establishment which Joe Crawhall and I shared was broken up, after two years, by my getting married. Joe was my best man, quite a new line of country for him but, like all his work, he did it truly and well.'[24]

In 1896, after his father's death, Crawhall returned to London to live with his mother and sister Beatrice. Crawhall's mother had never enjoyed living in the city and so, by 1898, they had moved to Aldfield, near Ripon. In 1899 they took a house named Beacon Banks in Husthwaite in Yorkshire where they lived for about three years before moving to Brandsby near Easingwold. Crawhall's mother leased Brandsby Hall from Mr Hugh Fairfax-Cholmeley, the squire of Brandsby, while their own home Dale End at the entrance to the village of Brandsby was completed. A plaque commemorating Crawhall remains *in situ* in Brandsby Hall recording his role as one of the hall's founders. According to Crawhall's biographer Adrian Bury, artist friends who visited Crawhall in Brandsby included Guthrie, Walton, Walter Russell, James Pryde, William Nicholson and the Rothensteins.[25] Crawhall's work may have influenced Russell, Nicholson and, in particular Pryde, who in 'his method of working . . . had much in common with Joseph Crawhall . . . whom he knew and greatly admired – and who is perhaps to be numbered among the artists who influenced his watercolours and pastels.'[26] These artist friends from Glasgow and London encouraged Crawhall to continue to paint and to exhibit. Russell described Crawhall's working practice at Brandsby: 'He had an essentially easy-going and inactive disposition, and then in a frenzy of creation would shut himself up in a room at the top of the house, which

119
Richard Walton
Joseph Crawhall on
Mesmuda in the Garden at
Beacon Banks
c.1899
Photograph

served as his unpretentious studio . . .' where he would ignore family, friends and meals until the work in hand was completed.[27]

Crawhall's life at Brandsby revolved around his art and his horses. Dale End had its own stables and his time would have been spent breeding hunters and racehorses and in hunting. His brother-in-law John Wood was land agent to the Cholmeley estate and shared his love of sport. Wood's son records the surprise of the sporting fraternity of the Brandsby neighbourhood at Crawhall's horsemanship but points out that few got to know him well because after attending a hunt, he would disappear before the social activities began.[28] While at Brandsby Crawhall is known to have hunted with the (North) York and Ainsty (South), the Sinnington and the Middleton.

His hunting experience and 'his lifelong addiction to horses and familiarity with sporting custom gave to his hunting pictures the stamp of truth.' Crawhall's paintings of meets 'brought a new dimension to sporting art and a breakaway

120
The Whip
c.1894–1900
Gouache on linen,
41.2×41.2
National Gallery of Scotland,
Edinburgh

from the stereotyped scenes of foxhunters streaming neatly across the pastures of the Shires.'[29] With the exception of *Following the Hounds* (pl 121), we rarely see a hunt itself in progress. Crawhall was not interested in capturing the movement of horses and riders across the terrain or in describing the countryside particular to each hunt. Instead, he concentrates on portraying the huntsman or the whip but although careful to render the pose of both horse and rider accurately, he is not interested in a finished portrait of either. *The Whip* (pl 120) is one of several similarly posed studies which suggest that Crawhall studied one figure from a series of differing angles. This is not peculiar to his hunting scenes, for there are at least three studies of a *Man on a Horse with a Dog Running Alongside* (Private Collections).

In *The Meet* (pl 122), the high horizon line contributes to the flattening of the picture plane in a way that is reminiscent of the startling design of George Henry's *A Galloway Landscape* (Glasgow Art Gallery and Museum). In *The Meet* the extensive use of gouache in the sky and grass show that this is an early work on linen. In his description of the horse in the foreground, however, we already have an example of a later more subtle technique. Here it is the linen that describes and defines the form and colour of the focal point of the composition, a technique used more successfully in *The Meet* (pl 123) where we look beyond the riders in the foreground down to the distant hills and dales of the Yorkshire countryside. Although no documentation survives about which hunt or which riders Crawhall

121
Following the Hounds
c.1898–1901
Gouache on linen,
16.0×21.5
Private Collection

123
The Meet
c.1894–8
Gouache on linen,
66.0×66.8
The Burrell Collection

122
The Meet
c.1894–8
Gouache on linen,
50.2×44.1
The Burrell Collection

124
The Huntsman
c.1894–8
Gouache on linen,
33.5×34.9
Glasgow Art Gallery and
Museum

so lovingly depicted, it is certain that despite his scant attention to facial features, these riders could have been identified by their contemporaries. Never intending a portrait Crawhall has, nevertheless, captured the individuality of the 'stern middle-aged matron with scarlet waistcoat on a rangy bay' in *The Meet* (pl 122).[30] Here too he has been concerned to show the effect of light on the landscape. The broad band of light, however, is used more to emphasise the abstract design of the composition than to record the effect of light on the landscape. A similar interest in design is seen in *The Huntsman* (pl 124) where we glimpse the huntsman and his pack through the autumn trees.

Crawhall, like Lavery and Cunninghame Graham, would have gone riding in London in The Row, which probably provides the setting for *In the Park* (pl 125). Once more a rider, as in *The Race*, is viewed from the back but, in this instance, it is an elegant lady seated side-saddle. *Four in Hand* (pl 126) was possibly also executed in London as the distant evening landscape suggests an urban setting. In a letter to Crawhall senior in 1890 Keene writes, 'I heard the assemblage in the

125
In the Park
c.1891
Watercolour on paper,
31.7×25.6
Private Collection

126
Four in Hand
c.1894
Gouache on linen,
33.0×40.0
Private Collection

Park at the four-in-hand meet was something tremendous. . . .'[31] *Four in Hand* is executed on a fine linen sparingly covered and with extensive areas of the textile left untouched. A pale green wash suffices to indicate the passing grass and all the warmth of colour is reserved for Crawhall's description of the horses with touches of yellow, orange, blue and terracotta. The horse and carriage as a means of transport was of equal fascination to Crawhall. In *The Flower Shop* (pl 127), *The Governess Cart* (Burrell Collection) and *Horse and Cart with Lady* (pl 128) Crawhall plays off the profiled curves of the horse against the lines and angular structure of the cart. *The Governess Cart* and *Horse and Cart with Lady* were

127
The Flower Shop
c.1894–1900
Gouache on linen,
28.2×35.2
The Burrell Collection

128
Horse and Cart with Lady
c.1894–1900
Gouache on linen,
24.3×32.6
Glasgow Art Gallery and
Museum

probably painted at Beacon Banks with his sister Beatrice as driver. The family's dachshund can just be glimpsed peeping out from behind her skirts in the latter – the same dog appearing in *Girl on Bicycle* (pl 130). The high viewpoint, the composition with its curving abstracted shape of the flower beds and the very theme of *Horse and Cart with Lady* make one feel certain that Crawhall had seen Degas's oil *Place de La Concorde, Paris* (destroyed).

By 1896 a new age was dawning where reliance on the horse would pass to reliance on the motor car. The sale of bicycles was booming and as one journalist put it capital 'to the amount of something like eleven millions went into cycling in 1896 alone; the Dunlop Pneumatic Tyre Company took five millions. The craze for the "pudding" tyre wheel . . . was swamping the manufacturers with orders, and new cycle company shares were – a little too late – as much a magnet for the mug's money in 1896 as gramophone record shares were in recent years. No one could dream of imminent punctures in rubber tyres, nor seriously visualise the upstarting of any mechanical vehicle to rival what was to become the poor man's carriage and the key to woman's emancipation.'[32] The bike boom burst in 1898 but not before Crawhall had captured his sister Beatrice in *Girl on Bicycle* wobbling her way uncertainly towards the viewer but still maintaining sufficient speed to cause the family dachshund to bounce alongside her in a near frenzy of face, tail and flying ears. An equally humorous reaction to new technology is seen in Crawhall's cartoon-like *The Road Hog* (pl 129). The determined driver and his passengers stare resolutely forward, seemingly unaware of the destruction the car has caused. Crawhall evidently shared the journalist Neil Munro's reaction to news of the benefits of the motor car: 'What a lot of bunkum is being talked and written about the motor car! It has been generally assumed that in a twelvemonth we shall be rushing across the landscape in weird puffs of paraffin fumes, and that the poor horse will only be available as a hatstand or a pen-wiper . . . the motor car of fact is a noisy, malodorous, uncertain, road locomotive, with more quirkiness of character than a mule, and diseases more unpleasant and costly to cure.'[33] Crawhall, the lover of animals, was still able to laugh at, and to capture succinctly the newfangled machinery that would eventually change the world as he had known it.

129
The Road Hog
c.1901–4
Watercolour on paper,
36.2×42.0
The Burrell Collection

130
Girl on Bicycle
c.1896
Watercolour on paper,
28.8×13.4
The Burrell Collection

EPILOGUE

It is known that Joseph Crawhall suffered lung trouble throughout his life – a condition not helped by his smoking and drinking. According to his obituarist in *The Times* he made a trip to London during the spring of 1913 'on business connected with the sale of some pictures.' He was staying at an hotel (possibly the Six Bells Tavern) in King's Road, Chelsea, when he was taken ill on 6 May. He was then moved to a nursing home in South Kensington and underwent an operation but died on 24 May, after the administration of the anaesthetic. The pathologist Dr Spilsbury was quoted in *The Times* as having revealed at the subsequent inquest that the artist had 'advanced disease of the heart, to which death was due, accelerated by the pneumonic condition of the lungs, and slightly accelerated by the anaesthetic.' The Coroner's verdict was 'Death by misadventure'.

Crawhall was buried at St Mary's Church, Morpeth, beside his father and his elder brother who had died in infancy. The *Morpeth Herald* carried details of the funeral: 'Enclosed in an oak coffin, the remains were conveyed by train from London overnight and placed in St. Mary's Church to await the internment in the afternoon. The Rev. Canon Davies, rector of Morpeth, conducted the burial service at the church and at the graveside.' The mourners included Sir James Guthrie, E. A. Walton and Abel Chapman. There were many wreaths: one from the dealer W. B. Paterson; another read 'In memory of J. Crawhall, member of the International Society of Sculptors, Painters, and Gravers'; and lastly 'To the deathless memory of a great artist, from Chelsea friends.'

Sir James Guthrie's words of tribute are testimony to the high regard in which Crawhall was held by his artist contemporaries. Guthrie wrote that, in his opinion, Crawhall 'has always been a consummate artist, the perfection of the means for the end he had in view, the fineness of his instinct for form, colour and design; the rare knowledge of life and movement and the even rarer application of that knowledge to an art of the most exacting sensitiveness and power – these things will always give him a unique place. Such a combination exists in none else known to me and his work throughout has in my mind borne the stamp of a master.' Sir John Lavery wrote that 'everything he did seemed to possess the value of a certain permanence', an opinion that was equally expressed in the obituary that appeared in *The Times* on 28 May: 'His work, unlike that of many artists who try to produce similar effects with slight effort, was the result of profound knowledge, elaborate care, and a keen sense both of colour and form; it therefore will have a permanent value.'

NOTES

1. THREE GENERATIONS

1. R. B. Cunninghame Graham, *Writ in Sand*, London, 1932, p. 82.
2. Ibid. p. 84. John Lavery, however, in his *The Life of a Painter*, London, 1940, p. 79, said that it was Cunninghame Graham who had given Crawhall the nickname.
3. A. Sutherland, *Joseph Crawhall – A Study in Artistic Development*, thesis submitted for BA, University of Durham, April 1935, p. 83.
4. Charles S. Felver, *Joseph Crawhall, The Newcastle Wood Engraver (1821–1896)*, Newcastle, 1972, p. 31.
5. Adrian Bury, *Joseph Crawhall, the Man and the Artist*, London, 1958, p. 25.
6. Quoted in Bury, op. cit. p. 25.
7. E. R. Forestier-Walker, *A History of the Wire Rope Industry of Great Britain*, London, 1952, p. 109.
8. Bury, op. cit. p. 28.
9. Felver, op. cit. pp. 7–8.
10. Quoted in Bury, op. cit. p. 28.
11. Private Collection.
12. Private Collection.
13. Forestier-Walker, op. cit. p. 110.
14. His collection was sold at Sotheby, Wilkinson and Hodge, on 22 and 23 June 1894.
15. Felver, op. cit. p. 63.
16. Ibid. p. 22.
17. Ibid. p. 23.
18. Ibid. p. 14.
19. Sutherland, op. cit. p. 11.
20. Ibid. p. 13.
21. A. H. Tweddle, *Town Trail for Morpethians*, no. 2, 1984, p. 9.
22. Sutherland, op. cit. p. 18.
23. Felver, op. cit. p. 83.
24. Joseph Crawhall, *Scrapbook 1887*, SL 920 C899. Central Library, Newcastle upon Tyne.
25. Collection: Glasgow Art Gallery and Museum.
26. George Somes Layard, *The Life and Letters of Charles Samuel Keene*, London, 1892, p. 192.
27. Ibid. p. 270.
28. *Local Biographies*, vol. 3, pp. 383–5, Central Library, Newcastle upon Tyne.
29. Felver, op. cit. p. 109.
30. Layard, op. cit. p. 282.
31. Ibid. pp. 244–5.
32. Ibid. p. 256.
33. Sutherland, op. cit. p. 24.
34. Layard, op. cit. pp. 274–5.
35. Ibid. p. 282.
36. Ibid. p. 285.
37. Ibid. pp. 292 and 301.
38. Ibid. p. 311.
39. Ibid. pp. 321, 336 and 346. There are further mentions in Layard, op. cit. pp. 358, 360, 363–4, 383 and 389.
40. Felver, op. cit. p. 81.
41. Layard, op. cit. p. 204.
42. Robert Robinson, *Thomas Bewick, His Life and Times*, 1888, p. 180.
43. Felver, op. cit. p. 67.
44. Ibid. p. 36.
45. The copy of the exhibition catalogue in the Central Library, Newcastle upon Tyne, previously belonged to Richard Walton, 40 Mosley Street, Newcastle upon Tyne.
46. *Newcastle Chronicle*, 20 April 1880, p. 113.
47. Ibid.
48. Quoted in Felver, op. cit. p. 91.

2. ONE OF THE BOYS

1. Macaulay Stevenson, Ms Notes, Collection: Mitchell Library, William Hardie Collection, f759. 2911 HAR.
2. James L. Caw, *Sir James Guthrie: A Biography*, London, 1932, p. xii.
3. Ibid. p. 7. Also mentioned in Frank Rinder, 'Sir James Guthrie P.R.S.A.', *The Art Journal*, 1911, p. 143.
4. An unidentified newspaper article of 1924 in the press-cuttings files of the Tate Archives, London.
5. Caw, op. cit. p. 8.
6. Ibid. Also quoted in Sutherland, op. cit. p. 31.
7. Caw, op. cit. p. 193. John Warrack in his memoir of Guthrie, printed in Caw's *Guthrie*, 1932, writes that Crawhall senior sent a telegram to Guthrie regarding the works for Newcastle that said, 'The picture was sent off and was hung on the line and sold on the opening day', p. 196.
8. Layard, op. cit. after p. 271.
9. Caw, op. cit. p. 213, suggests other works on which the two might have collaborated: *South Shields* (11½ × 7½); *The Bridge, Crowland* (12 × 9½). Crawhall and his sister posed for Guthrie's *Tête-à-Tête*, 1882 (Private Collection).
10. Sutherland, op. cit. pp. 32–5.
11. Quoted in Felver, op. cit. p. 29.
12. Letter from Guthrie to Lavery, 7245/15 in the Tate Archives, London.
13. Letter from Crawhall to Walton, D.5102/39 in the National Gallery of Scotland, Edinburgh.
14. A. S. Hartrick, *A Painter's Pilgrimage through Fifty Years*, Cambridge, 1939, p. 58.
15. A. Stodart Walker, 'Sir James Guthrie P.R.S.A.', *The Studio*, vol. LIV, 1912, p. 21.
16. *Scottish Art Review*, November 1988, p. 146.
17. Introduction by Stanley Cursiter in catalogue of Paterson Memorial Exhibition, Scottish Gallery, Edinburgh.
18. Lavery, op. cit. p. 108.
19. *St Paul's Magazine*, 18 June 1898.
20. Layard, op. cit. 24 May 1878, p. 269.
21. Lavery, op. cit. p. 79.
22. Obituary of Joseph Crawhall in *Morning Post*, 27 May 1913.

23. Caw, op. cit. pp. 22–3.
24. Letter, Collection: the Fine Art Society, London.
25. James L. Caw, 'A Scottish Painter: E. A. Walton A.R.S.A.', *The Studio*, vol. 26, 1902, p. 168.
26. E. A. Taylor, 'The Development of British Landscape Painting in Watercolour: Scottish Painters', in *Studio Special Number*, no. 78, 1918, p. 31.
27. Hartrick, op. cit. p. 58.
28. *Scottish Art Review*, no. 19, December 1889, p. 221.
29. Caw, *Guthrie*, p. 51.
30. *Westminster Gazette*, 4 February 1893, quoted in A. E. Mackay, *Arthur Melville, Scottish Impressionist, 1855–1904*, Leigh-on-Sea, 1951, p. 71.
31. Letter, 25 December 1890. In *Joseph Crawhall Letters 1833–1896*, L761, Central Library, Newcastle upon Tyne.
32. *St. Louis Life*, 14 September 1895. In Hornel press-cuttings book, Broughton House, Kirkcudbright.
33. With the notable exception of James L. Caw. See James L. Caw, *Scottish Painting Past and Present 1620–1908*, London, 1908, p. 438. See also James L. Caw, 'A Phase of Scottish Art', *The Art Journal*, 1894, p. 80.
34. Lavery, op. cit. p. 79.

3. TANGIER AND SPAIN

1. H. T. Finck, *Spain and Morocco: Studies in Local Colour*, New York, 1891, p. 77.
2. *The Journal of Eugène Delacroix*, edited by Hubert Wellington, London, 1951, p. 53.
3. William Kennedy settled in Tangier in 1912 and died there in 1918.
4. Sutherland, op. cit. p. 53.
5. Cunninghame Graham, op. cit. p. 84.
6. Layard, op. cit. p. 308.
7. Ibid. p. 346.
8. Cunninghame Graham, op. cit. pp. 121–2.
9. Letter, 14 February 1888. In *Joseph Crawhall Letters 1833–1896*, L761, Central Library, Newcastle upon Tyne.

10. Ibid. Letters, 25 March and 17 April 1889.
11. Martin Hopkinson, *Alexander Mann 1853–1908, Sketches and Correspondence with His Wife and Family*, Fine Art Society, London, n.d.
12. Finck, op. cit. p. 78.
13. Edmondo De Amicis, *Morocco, Its People and Places*, 2 vols., Philadelphia, 1897, vol. I, p. 7.
14. Ibid. p. 5.
15. Ibid. p. 72.
16. Lavery, op. cit. p. 98.
17. Finck, op. cit. p. 83ff.
18. *Saturday Review*, 1 October 1904.
19. Mackay, op. cit. p. 66.
20. Ibid. p. 115.
21. *The Scottish Review*, 3 October 1907, quoted in Mackay, op. cit. p. 65.
22. Mackay, op. cit. pp. 26–7.
23. *Daily Chronicle*, 24 June 1883, quoted in Mackay, op. cit. p. 61.
24. Caw, *Scottish Painting*, p. 397.
25. Major-General Lord Edward Gleichen, *A Guardsman's Memories, A Book of Recollections*, Edinburgh and London, 1932, p. 124.
26. *The Newcastle Journal*, 30 June 1888.
27. Lavery, op. cit. p. 89.
28. Cunninghame Graham, op. cit. pp. 81–2.
29. Ibid. pp. 123–6.
30. George Denholm Armour, *Bridle and Brush, Reminiscences of an Artist Sportsman*, London and New York, 1936, p. 94.
31. G. D. Armour, 'The Lighter Side of a Great Artist. Some Memories of Joseph Crawhall', *The Connoisseur*, vol. XCIII, December 1936, pp. 322–7.
32. G. D. Armour, *Bridle and Brush*, p. 97.
33. Bury saw the Cup in the collection of Crawhall's nephew J. E. C. Wood.
34. Gleichen, op. cit. p. 125.
35. G. D. Armour, *Bridle and Brush*, p. 95.
36. Frias, 'After Tangier Pig', *Pall Mall Magazine*, vol. 20, 1901, pp. 485–90.
37. Lavery, op. cit. p. 57.
38. *Sir John Lavery RA, 1856–1941*,

exhibition catalogue by Kenneth McConkey, the Fine Art Society and the Ulster Museum, Belfast, 1984, p. 29.
39. Walter Shaw-Sparrow, *John Lavery and His Work*, London, 1911, pp. 86–7.
40. Lavery, op. cit. p. 81.
41. Ibid. p. 76.
42. The German artist Auguste Neven du Mont gave £500 to assist with the second exhibition of the International Society of Sculptors, Painters and Gravers. Lavery, op. cit. p. 111.
43. Card, 14 June 1903, 7245/110, Tate Archives, London.
44. Lavery, op. cit. p. 128.
45. Ibid. p. 77.
46. Sutherland, op. cit. p. 73.
47. G. D. Armour, *Bridle and Brush*, p. 115.
48. Lavery, op. cit. p. 101.
49. G. D. Armour, *Bridle and Brush*, p. 127.
50. Sutherland, op. cit. pp. 72–3.

4. EXHIBITIONS, COLLECTORS AND DEALERS

1. David Martin, 'Some Paintings by Joseph Crawhall Jun.', *The Studio*, vol. III, no. 18, 1894, p. 166.
2. Cunninghame Graham, op. cit. p. 87.
3. *The Times*, 28 May 1913.
4. Letter from Ian McNicol to A. J. McNeill Reid of 29 November 1965. National Library of Scotland.
5. Layard, op. cit. p. 311.
6. Frank Rinder, 'Joseph Crawhall', *Art Journal*, 1911, p. 71, and in *Morning Post*, 27 May 1913.
7. Letters from Joseph Crawhall to Alexander Reid. Collection: Acc 9787 National Library of Scotland.
8. Gleichen, op. cit. p. 125.
9. Felver, op. cit. p. 39.
10. Layard, op. cit. p. 311.
11. Felver, op. cit. p. 77.
12. Felver, op. cit. p. 89.
13. Acc 9787 National Library of Scotland.
14. Ibid.
15. Ibid.
16. Ibid.
17. Caw, *Guthrie*, p. 73.

18. *The Bailie*, 19 December 1877, p. 10.
19. It became the Royal Society of Painters in Watercolours in 1888.
20. Archives of the Royal Scottish Society of Painters in Watercolours.
21. A letter in *Joseph Crawhall Letters 1833–1896*, L761, Central Library, Newcastle upon Tyne, suggests Crawhall had some drawings accepted at the 'Academy' in 1886 but that they were not hung.
22. *Glasgow Herald*, 4 November 1887, p. 8.
23. *Scottish Art Review*, vol. I, November 1888, pp. 153–4.
24. *Glasgow Herald*, 6 November 1891, p. 4.
25. *The Studio*, vol. I, 1893, p. 211.
26. The books containing the Minutes of the International Society of Sculptors, Painters and Gravers are held in the Tate Archives, London. The particular books consulted are 738. 1–4.
27. Letter of 18 July 1903, 7245/58 in the Tate Archives, London.
28. *Glasgow Evening Citizen*, 16 May 1896.
29. Philip Athill, 'The International Society of Sculptors, Painters and Gravers', *The Burlington Magazine*, November 1985, p. 26.
30. A series of press-cutting books containing reviews of the International Society exhibitions are in the National Art Library, Victoria and Albert Museum, London.
31. *Brighton Society*, 21 May 1898.
32. *St. Paul's Magazine*, 18 June 1898.
33. *The Athenaeum*, 23 January 1904.
34. Alfred Thornton, *Fifty Years of the New English Art Club 1886–1935*, London, 1935, pp. 3 and 13.
35. Glasgow Boy members included: Guthrie (1889–93), Henry (1889–91), Lavery (1889–93), Walton (1888–93) and Mann (1888–93).
36. Letter from William Burrell to A. J. McNeill Reid, quoted in Scottish Arts Council, *A Man of Influence: Alex Reid*, exhibition catalogue by Ronald Pickvance, Glasgow, 1967, p. 5.
37. Pickvance, op. cit. p. 15.
38. Acc 9787 National Library of Scotland, Edinburgh.
39. Ibid.
40. Ibid.
41. Ibid.
42. John F. Barclay, *Arthur and Company Ltd., One Hundred Years of Textile Distribution*, Glasgow, 1953.
43. T.C.M., 'The Crawhalls of Mr. William Burrell's Collection', *The Studio*, vol. 83, April, 1922, p. 177.
44. Letter from William Burrell to Mr Aitken, 13 December 1927, Tate Archives, London.
45. Richard Marks, *Burrell, A Portrait of a Collector, Sir William Burrell 1861–1958*, Glasgow, 1983, p. 72.
46. Bury, op. cit. p. 20.
47. Information on A. Reid sales to Glasgow collectors can be found in Acc. 6925 in the National Library of Scotland, Edinburgh.
48. T. J. Honeyman, *Art and Audacity*, Glasgow, 1971, p. 125.
49. Acc. 6925, National Library of Scotland, Edinburgh.
50. Letter in the Burrell Collection, 35/151.
51. *The Times*, 17 May 1912, p. 10.

5. HUMOURIST AND ILLUSTRATOR

1. Bury, op. cit. p. 109.
2. Ibid. pp. 71–2.
3. Layard, op. cit. p. 303.
4. Hartrick, op. cit. p. 100.
5. David Cuppleditch, *Phil May – The Artist and His Wit*, London, 1981, p. 87.
6. Caw, *Guthrie*, p. 19.
7. Felver, op. cit. pp. 81–2.
8. Abel Chapman and Walter J. Buck, *Unexplored Spain*, London, 1910, p. 1.
9. Ibid. p. 43.
10. Sutherland, op. cit. p. 121.
11. *The History of Reynard the Fox*, translated and printed by William Caxton in 1481, edited and with an introduction by Donald B. Sands, London, 1960, p. 3.
12. I am indebted to Professor K. Varty of the University of Glasgow for introducing me to the history of Reynard the Fox. Much of the information here was first suggested by Professor Varty but the author is solely responsible for any mistakes.
13. Sands, op. cit. p. 45.
14. Ibid. p. 46.
15. Ibid. p. 48.
16. Ibid. pp. 51–2.
17. Ibid. p. 54.
18. Ibid. p. 56.
19. Ibid. p. 58.
20. Ibid. p. 64.
21. Ibid. p. 65.
22. Ibid. p. 67.
23. Ibid. p. 76.
24. Ibid. p. 108.
25. Ibid. p. 99.
26. Ibid. p. 109.
27. Kenneth Varty, *Reynard the Fox*, Leicester, 1967, p. 91.
28. Sands, op. cit. pp. 116–17.
29. Ibid. p. 157.
30. Ibid. p. 186.

6. A LOVE OF ANIMALS

1. Lavery, op. cit. p. 82.
2. Bury, op. cit. p. 83.
3. Macaulay Stevenson, op. cit.
4. Frank Rinder, 'Joseph Crawhall', *The Art Journal*, 1911, p. 75.
5. The Annual Reports of the British Zoological Gardens are preserved in the archives of the Zoo at Clifton, Bristol.
6. Fifty-seventh Report, 1893, p. 7.
7. Bury, op. cit. frontispiece text.
8. Cunninghame Graham, op. cit. pp. 85–6.
9. Essay on 'Barnet Fair' by Hilary Thomas in *Historic Barnet*, London, p. 45.
10. Ibid. pp. 47–8.
11. Father Barnfield, *Early Barnet Recollections*, London, 1899, pp. 23–4.
12. Ibid. p. 23.
13. Sutherland, op. cit. p. 101.
14. Ibid. pp. 98–9.
15. Bury, op. cit. p. 97.
16. Introduction by H. G. Hutchinson in G. D. Armour, *Pastime with Good Company*, London, n.d., p. 1.

17. Mackay, op. cit. p. 66, has, 'In many ways he [Crawhall] resembled Degas. Both in drawing and painting he expressed a sort of natural synthesis, and had a Degas-like faculty of suggesting movement and light'. A. J. McNeill Reid in a draft letter writes, 'I would place Crawhall in your correspondents second category of little, but not so very little, master who knew his limitations. He can certainly not be ranked with Degas but he had the faculty of portraying animals in movement in a way that Degas himself rarely equalled'. Letter in ACC 6925/iv, National Library of Scotland, Edinburgh.

18. From the title page of *The Third Tour of Dr Syntax in Search of a Wife*, 1821.

19. A letter from Crawhall senior to his sister Mary, in *Joseph Crawhall Letters 1833–1886*, L761, Central Library, Newcastle upon Tyne. 'Joe and fellow artist [Armour] have taken a country home about twenty five miles north of London – Wheathamstead a few miles north of Hatfield and St Albans, where they intend setting to work in earnest and I'm glad to say Joe finds a ready sale and good (–) for all he produces . . .'.

20. G. D. Armour, *Bridle and Brush*, pp. 139–40.

21. Ibid. pp. 142–3.

22. Ibid. pp. 145–6.

23. Caw, *Scottish Painting*, p. 465.

24. G. D. Armour, op. cit. p. 149.

25. Bury, op. cit. p. 75.

26. Derek Hudson, *James Pryde 1866–1941*, London, 1949, p. 75.

27. Bury, op. cit. p. 76.

28. Bury, op. cit. p. 75.

29. S. A. Walker, 'Unfamiliar names in the world of sporting art', *Horse and Hound*, 1 March 1974, p. 37.

30. Ibid. p. 92.

31. Layard, op. cit. p. 419.

32. Neil Munro, *The Brave Days, A Chronicle from the North*, Edinburgh, 1931, p. 126.

33. Ibid. p. 125.

BIBLIOGRAPHY

Major printed sources are given below. There is, however, a wealth of unpublished material relating to exhibitions and collectors in the archives of the many exhibiting bodies. Press-cuttings books for exhibitions of the period 1880–1920 can be consulted in the Special Collections Department, Glasgow University Library; the National Art Library, Victoria and Albert Museum; and the Tate Archives, London. There is a John Lavery archive in the Tate Archives, London; Macaulay Stevenson's MS notes are in the Mitchell Library, Glasgow; E. A. Walton's papers and some of the papers of Alexander Reid are in the Manuscript Department of the National Library of Scotland. The major British collection of manuscripts and books relating to the Crawhall family is held in the Local Studies Department, Central Library, Newcastle upon Tyne.

GENERAL WORKS

Alex Reid and Lefevre, 1926–1976, The Lefevre Gallery. Introduction by Douglas Cooper.

Athill, Philip, 'The International Society of Sculptors, Painters and Gravers', *Burlington Magazine*, November 1985, pp. 21–9.

Billcliffe, Roger, *The Glasgow Boys, The Glasgow School of Painting 1875–1895*, London, 1985.

Bird, Elizabeth, 'International Glasgow', *The Connoisseur*, vol. 83, August 1973, pp. 248–57.

Brown, Gerard Baldwin, *The Glasgow School of Painters*, Glasgow, 1908.

Burnand, Sir F. C., 'Artists on Horseback', *Art Journal*, February 1909, pp. 33–40.

Bury, Adrian, *Two Centuries of British Watercolour Painting*, London, 1950.

Caw, Sir James Lewis, *Scottish Painting: Past and Present 1620–1908*, Edinburgh, 1908.

—— 'A Phase of Scottish Art', *Art Journal*, 1894, pp. 75–80.

The Fine Art Society, *The Glasgow School of Painting*. Exhibition catalogue and introduction by William R. Hardie, London, 1970.

—— *Glasgow 1900*. Exhibition catalogue and introduction by Roger Billcliffe; introductory essay by Elizabeth Bird, Glasgow, 1979.

Hardie, Martin, *Water-colour Painting in Britain*: vol. III, *The Victorian Period*, London, 1968.

Hardie, William R., *Scottish Painting, 1837–1939*, London, 1976.

Irwin, David and Francina, *Scottish Painters: At Home and Abroad 1700–1900*, London, 1975.

MacColl, D. S., 'The New English Art Club', *The Studio*, March 1945, pp. 65–73.

McConkey, Kenneth, 'From Grez to Glasgow: French Naturalist Influence in Scottish Painting', *Scottish Art Review*, vol. XV, no. 4, November 1982, pp. 16–34.

Martin, David, *The Glasgow School of Painting*, London, 1897.

Munro, Neil, *The Brave Days*, Edinburgh, 1931.

Muther, Richard, *History of Modern Painting*, English translation, 4 vols., London, 1895–6.

Robinson, Robert, *Thomas Bewick, His Life and Times*, Newcastle, 1888.

Rothenstein, William, *Men and Memories: Recollections of William Rothenstein*, 2 vols., London, 1931 and 1932.

Scottish Arts Council, *The Glasgow Boys*. Exhibition catalogue by William Buchanan and others; two vols., Edinburgh, 1968 and 1971.

—— *A Man of Influence: Alex Reid*. Exhibition catalogue by Ronald Pickvance, Glasgow, 1967.

Varty, Kenneth, *Reynard the Fox*, Leicester, 1967.

BOOKS AND ARTICLES ON JOSEPH CRAWHALL
(listed in chronological order)

Martin, David, 'Some Paintings by Joseph Crawhall Jun.', *The Studio*, vol. 3, September 1894, pp. 166–70.

Frias, 'After Tangier Pig', *Pall Mall Magazine*, vol. 20, 1901, pp. 485–90.

Bate, Percy, 'Joseph Crawhall, Master Draughtsman', *The Studio*, vol. 32, 1904.

X, '*North Country Artist and His Work – Joseph Crawhall, Master Draughtsman*', *Border Magazine*, 1904, pp. 127–8.

Keudell, Baronin von, 'Joseph Crawhall', *Kunst und Kunsthandwerk*, vol. 8, 1905, pp. 1–7.

Rinder, Frank, 'Joseph Crawhall', *Art Journal*, 1911, pp. 71–7.

Simpson, James Shaw, 'Joseph Crawhall: The Man and His Work', *Scottish Country Life*, July 1916, pp. 306–7.

T.C.M., 'The Crawhalls of Mr William Burrell's Collection', *The Studio*, April 1922, vol. 83, pp. 177–86.

Sutherland, A., *Joseph Crawhall (1861–1913) – A Study in Artistic Development*. BA thesis submitted to the University of Durham, 1935.

Armour, George Denholm, 'The Lighter Side of a Great Artist. Some Memories of Joseph Crawhall', *Connoisseur*, vol. 93, December 1936, pp. 322–7.

Hardie, Martin, 'Joseph Crawhall', *The Old Watercolour Society's Club*, vol. 23, 1945, pp. 28–35.
Bury, Adrian, 'The Genius of Joseph Crawhall', *The British Racehorse*, June 1955, pp. 120–5.
——— 'Joseph Crawhall', *Apollo*, November 1957, pp. 112–16.
——— *Joseph Crawhall, the Man and the Artist*, London, 1958.
Davis, Frank, 'A Page for Collectors: The Great Silence', *Illustrated London News*, 21 February 1959, p. 306.
Neve, Christopher, 'Drawn from Memory: Joseph Crawhall', *Country Life*, 1 May 1969, pp. 1088–9.
——— 'Joseph Crawhall as Horse Painter', *The British Racehorse*, October 1969, pp. 380–9.
Felver, Charles S., *Joseph Crawhall, The Newcastle Wood Engraver (1821–1896)*, Newcastle, 1972.
Walker, Stella A., 'Unfamiliar Names in the World of Sporting Art', *Horse and Hound*, 1 March 1974, pp. 37 and 92.
Hall, Marshall, *The Artists of Northumbria*, Newcastle upon Tyne, 2nd ed. 1982.
Houfe, Simon, 'Extracting the Honey: Charles Keene and Joseph Crawhall', *Antiquarian Book Monthly Review*, February 1984, pp. 44–9.

CRAWHALL'S CONTEMPORARIES

ALEXANDER, Edwin
Patterson, James, 'Edwin Alexander 1870–1926', *Old Watercolour Society Club*, 4th Annual volume, 1926–7, pp. 53–66.

ARMOUR, George Denholm
Armour, George Denholm, *The Humours of Sport*, London, 1905.
——— *Humour in the Hunting Field*, London, 1928.
——— *A Hunting Alphabet*, London, 1929.
——— *Pastime with Good Company*, London, n.d.
——— *Sport – And There's the Humour of it*, London, n.d.
——— *Bridle and Brush, Reminiscences of an Artist Sportsman*, London, 1937.

CHAPMAN, Abel
Chapman, Abel, and Buck, Walter J., *Unexplored Spain*, London, 1910.
Chapman, Abel, *Retrospect: Reminiscences of a Hunter – Naturalist in Three Continents 1851–1928*, London, 1928.

CUNNINGHAME GRAHAM, R. B.
Cunninghame Graham, R. B., *Writ in Sand*, London, 1932.

GUTHRIE, Sir James
Rinder, Frank, 'Sir James Guthrie PRSA', *Art Journal*, 1911, pp. 139–44 and 270–5.
Walker, A. Stodart, 'Portraits by Sir James Guthrie PRSA', *The Studio*, vol. 54, 1912, pp. 18–26.
Caw, Sir James Lewis, *Sir James Guthrie PRSA LLD: A Biography*, London, 1932.
The Fine Art Society, *Guthrie and the Scottish Realists*, Glasgow, 1982. Exhibition catalogue by Roger Billcliffe.

HARTRICK, Archibald Standish
Hartrick, A. S., *A Painter's Pilgrimage through Fifty Years*, Cambridge, 1939.

KEENE, Charles
Layard, George Somes, *The Life and Letters of Charles Samuel Keene*, London, 1892.
Hudson, Derek, *Charles Keene*, London, 1947.

LAVERY, Sir John
Shaw-Sparrow, Walter, *John Lavery and His Work*, London, 1911.
Lavery, John, *The Life of a Painter*, London, 1940.
University of St Andrews, *John Lavery: The Early Career, 1880–1895*, 1983. Exhibition catalogue by David Scruton.
The Fine Art Society and the Ulster Museum, Belfast, *Sir John Lavery RA, 1856–1941*, 1984. Exhibition catalogue by Kenneth McConkey, contains a complete bibliography of Lavery.

MANN, Alexander
The Fine Art Society, *Alexander Mann*, 1983. Exhibition catalogue; introduction by Christopher Newall.
——— *Alexander Mann 1853–1908; Sketches and Correspondence with His Wife and Family*. Foreword by Martin Hopkinson, London, n.d.

MAY, Phil
Cuppleditch, David, *Phil May: The Artist and His Wit*, London, 1981.

MELVILLE, Arthur
Mackay, Agnes Ethel, *Arthur Melville, Scottish Impressionist, 1855–1904*, Leigh-on-Sea, 1951.
Dundee Art Gallery, *Arthur Melville*, 1977. Exhibition catalogue by Gerald Deslandes.

MOROT, Aimé
Moreau-Vauthier, M. Ch., *L'Oeuvre de Aimé Morot*, Paris, 1906.

WALTON, Edward Arthur
Caw, Sir James Lewis, 'A Scottish Painter', *The Studio*, vol. 26, 1902, pp. 161–70.
Macsporran, Fiona, *Edward Arthur Walton 1860–1922*, Glasgow, 1987.

TANGIER

Finck, Henry T., *Spain and Morocco: Studies in Local Colour*, New York, 1891.
De Amicis, Edmondo, *Morocco, Its People and Places*, 2 vols., Philadelphia, 1897.
Gastin, Norman, 'Tangier as a sketching ground', *The Studio*, vol. 53, August 1897, pp. 177–82.
Cunninghame Graham, R. B., 'The Atmosphere of Morocco', *Sketching Grounds, The Studio Special Number*, 1909.
Gleichen, Major-General Lord Edward, *A Guardsman's Memories. A Book of Recollections*, Edinburgh and London, 1932.

APPENDIX 1: LIST OF EXHIBITIONS, 1878–1940

Works by Joseph Crawhall were seen in many exhibitions in Britain during the period 1878–1940. Only information from catalogues which I have been able to consult at first hand is included here. I am aware that works by the artist were included in many other exhibitions and would be grateful to learn of the whereabouts of these catalogues.

Crawhall's place in the history of Scottish Art was firmly established with the exhibition of Scottish Art at the Royal Academy, London, in 1939. It seemed appropriate, therefore, to end the exhibition listing with the exhibition of British Painting held at the National Gallery in 1940. Two later exhibitions of importance were: Crawhall in the Burrell Collection (Glasgow, 1953) and the Centenary Exhibition of Paintings and Drawings by Joseph Crawhall, the Reid Gallery, London, 1961.

1878

Arts Association, Newcastle upon Tyne

September–November

| n 54 | Fox Hounds – Morpeth | |
| n 321 | A Collie Dog | |

1879

Arts Association, Newcastle upon Tyne

Autumn (September–October)

n 191	Head of Lioness (from life)	£10 10s.
n 208	Cinderella	£10 10s.
n 218	The Sentinels	£12 12s.

1880

Arts Association, Newcastle upon Tyne

Spring (loan and sale)

n 250	Bolted (Joseph Crawhall Jnr. and J. E. Guthrie)	For sale
n 268	Drowsy	For sale
n 292	Calf (from life)	For sale

Arts Association, Newcastle upon Tyne

Autumn

| n 250 | Sleeping Dog | £6 |

1881

Arts Association, Newcastle upon Tyne

Autumn

| n 111 | Study of Trout | £5 5s. |
| n 486 | A Caution | £4 4s. |

1882

Glasgow Institute of the Fine Arts

21st

| n 131 | Disappointment | £10 |

1883

Royal Academy, London

| n 161 | A Lincolnshire Pasture | |

Glasgow Institute of the Fine Arts

22nd

| n 583 | Cloot Drain, Lincolnshire | £12 12s. |

1886

Scottish Society of Painters in Watercolours, Glasgow

9th

n 4	Dick	£16 16s.
n 115	A White Horse	£12 12s.
n 509	The Duck Pond	£8 8s.

1887

Scottish Society of Painters in Watercolours, Glasgow

10th

n 45	A Pasture near the Sea	£10 10s.
n 95	Left in Charge	£12 12s.
n 145	Harriers	£14 14s.
n 157	Study at La Villette	£13 13s.
n 161	A Veteran	£15 15s.
n 171	A Garden Path	£8 8s.
n 184	The Forge	£22 10s.
n 216	Pigeons	£15 15s.
n 297	Illustrations	£30

1888

Scottish Society of Painters in Watercolours, Glasgow

11th

n 37	Goats	£18
n 40	Moorish Packhorse	£18
n 187	Sok, Tangier	£16
n 218	A Snake Charmer – Morocco	£35
n 240	In the Fondak of Sebastian	£18
n 274	Moorish Donkeys	£8
n 279	Camels	£8

International Exhibition, Glasgow

| n 1014 | A Veteran | £15 15s. |

1889

Royal Scottish Society of Painters in Watercolours, Glasgow

12th

n 28	In the Bull Ring, Algeciras	£30
n 122	Bullfighters, Algeciras	£20
n 177	In the Aviary, Clifton	W. B. Paterson

1890

New English Art Club, London

5th, March–May

| n 70 | In the Parrot House | NFS |

1891

Glasgow East End Industrial Exhibition

| n 310 | Hen and Chickens | James Garroway |

Royal Scottish Society of Painters in Watercolours, Glasgow

14th

n 194	Spanish Bullfight	NFS
n 195	Spanish Bullfight	NFS
n 196	In the Stable	NFS

1892

Autumn Exhibition of Modern Art, Liverpool

22nd

| n 782 | The Bullfight | |
| n 783 | Pigeons | |

1893

Grafton Galleries, London

n 249	The Greyhound	
n 254	Interior of a Smithy	
n 254a	The Bullfight	

Royal Scottish Society of Painters in Watercolours, Edinburgh

16th

n 221	A Hound Asleep	£25
n 401	Bullfight at Algeciras	NFS
n 407	Interior of a Circus	NFS

1893

The Collected Works of Joseph Crawhall
Alexander Reid
La Société des Beaux-Arts,
124 St Vincent Street, Glasgow

Eighty works listed – see Appendix 2

1895

Glasgow Institute of the Fine Arts

34th

| n 601 | The Circus | George Burrell |
| n 602 | Rabbit | George Burrell |

1898

International Society of Sculptors, Painters and Gravers, London

1st

n 285	The Black Cock	
n 286	Pigeon	
n 287	The Whip	
n 288	Performing Dogs	
n 289	The Huntsman	
n 291	Wild Doves in a Cage	
n 292	The Black Rabbit	

1899

Paisley Art Institute

23rd, March–April

| n 199 | The Snake Charmer | George Burrell |

International Society of Painters, Sculptors and Gravers, London

2nd, May–July

n 223	The Farmer's Boy	T. N. Whitelaw
n 224	Huntsmen and Hounds	H. H. Smiley
n 225	A Horse Fair	
n 226	Bullfight at Algeciras	William Burrell

1901

International Exhibition, Glasgow

n 695	Cockatoo	William Burrell
n 1067	The Pigeon	William Burrell
n 1070	Black Cock	William Burrell
n 1072	Black Rabbit	George Burrell

International Society of Sculptors, Painters and Gravers, London

3rd, October–December

n 7   The Jackdaw
n 23   Barnet Fair

Whitechapel Art Gallery, London

n 341   The Circus   James Gardiner
n 342   The Smithy   James Gardiner

1902

Paisley Art Institute

28th, December–January 1903

n 267   The Hansom Cab   Thomas Dunlop

1903

Royal Glasgow Institute of the Fine Arts

42nd

n 426   The Piebald   John Nairn

1904

International Society of Sculptors, Painters and Gravers, London

4th, January–March

n 44   Silver Spangled Cock

1905

Contemporary Artists of the English and Scottish Schools
W. B. Paterson, 5 Old Bond Street, London

February–March

n 7   The Aviary
n 8   The Black Cock
n 16   A Paris Cab
n 19   The Rabbits

Royal Glasgow Institute of the Fine Arts

44th

n 589   Pigeons   J. A. Holms
n 616   Jackdaw with Peacock's Feathers J. A. Holms
n 620   The Farmer's Boy   John Keppie

1906

Drawings in Watercolour and Black and White
W. B. Paterson, 5 Old Bond Street, London

April

n 19   Hunting Scene
n 22   The Tiger
n 26   The White Drake
n 27   Grey Horse
n 30   The Chinese Goose

and A Set of 10 Drawings representing Scenes from the Fable of Reynarde ye Foxe

n 20   Rukenawe the She Ape Counsels the Foxe
n 21   How Bruyn the Bere ate the Hony
n 23   The Foxe and the Capone
n 24   Tybert the Catte in the Gryn

n 25   Courtoys the Hounde
n 28   Ysegrym the Wulf and the Mare
n 29   Corbant the Roke and Reynarde
n 31   The Fox and the Wulf's Wyf
n 32   Bellyn the Ramme, Kywart the Hare, and
       Reynarde the Foxe

A note in the catalogue continues 'The Ten Drawings by J. Crawhall illustrating the Fable of "Reynard the Fox" are being reproduced in fac-simile, and will be ready for publication in a few months' time. The issue will be strictly limited to two hundred sets, and the price is Ten Guineas net. Two specimen proofs are included in the present exhibition. Mr. Paterson will be glad to receive names of intending subscribers.'

1907

International Society of Sculptors, Painters and Gravers, London

7th, January–March

n 58   The Magpie
n 63   The Pheasant
n 73   The Whipper-In
n 306   The White Drake

Exhibition of Watercolour Drawings
W. B. Paterson, 5 Old Bond Street, London

May

n 14   Mare and Foal
n 16   Lady on Horseback Attended by Groom
n 18   The Old Hunter
n 24   North American Indian
n 25   The Horsepond

The facsimile series, Reynard the Fox, was included in this exhibition.

Whitechapel Art Gallery, London

n 79   Hunting Scene   John Macintyre
n 80   Canary   John Macintyre

1908

Exhibition of Watercolour Drawings
W. B. Paterson, 5 Old Bond Street, London

March–April

n 25   The Moorhen
n 26   An Arab Donkey
n 27   Bullfinches
n 28   Trout Rising
n 34   The Gentleman Farmer
n 35   Pig-Sticking

1909

International Society of Sculptors, Painters and Gravers, London

9th, January–February

n 9   The Mallard
n 67   The Circus Rider

New English Art Club, London

41st, Summer

n 298   The Farmer's Boy
n 301   The Magpie
n 302   The Pheasant
n 303   The Chinese Goose
n 304   The Picador
n 320   The Paris Cab

New English Art Club, London

42nd, Winter

n 216   The Horse Pond
n 217   The Coach
n 219   The Rook's Nest
n 221   The Elephant

Royal Scottish Society of Painters in Watercolours, Edinburgh

30th

n 22   Spangled Cock   J. A. Holms
n 161   Pigeons   J. A. Holms

Royal Glasgow Institute of the Fine Arts

48th

n 394   The Bullring   Archibald Robertson

Autumn Exhibition of Modern Art, Liverpool

39th

n 523   The Bullring   Archibald Robertson
n 1446   A Jockey

1910

New English Art Club, London

43rd

n 132   The Cock

Whitechapel Art Gallery, London

n 343   Feeding Time   John Keppie
n 359   Dogs   Mrs R. Paton
n 423   Horses   J. R. Kinghorn
n 428   Dove in a Cage   F. Rowntree

1911

International Society of Sculptors, Painters and Gravers, London. Century of Art Exhibition 1810–1910 Grafton Galleries

June–July

n 302   The Magpie
n 307   The Spangled Cock

Autumn Exhibition of Modern Art, Liverpool

41st

n 559   The Performing Elephant

Paisley Art Institute

36th, December–January 1912

n 147   Race Horses   W. A. Coats

1912

Loan Collection of Watercolour Drawings by Joseph Crawhall
W. B. Paterson, 5 Old Bond Street, London

May–June

Fifty works listed – see Appendix 2

Autumn Exhibition of Modern Art, Liverpool

42nd

n 429   The Performing Dogs   W. A. Coats
n 438   The Magpie   W. A. Coats
n 630   The White Horse   John P. Currie
n 638   The Mallard   W. A. Coats

Grosvenor Gallery, London

October

n 77   The Picador
n 85   The Cow

New English Art Club, London

48th Winter

n 64   The Butcher's Boy

Royal Scottish Society of Painters in Watercolours, Edinburgh

33rd

n 65   Bullfight   Archibald Robertson
n 158   The Meet   John Tattersall

Loan Collection, Victoria Art Galleries, Dundee

n 77   The Rook's Nest   John Robertson

1913

Autumn Exhibition of Modern Art, Liverpool

43rd

n 540   Pigeons   W. G. Gardiner

Royal Glasgow Institute of the Fine Arts

52nd

n 503   The Magpie   W. A. Coats
n 531   The White Drake   W. A. Coats
n 576   A Huntsman   Lady Smiley

1914

International Society of Painters, Sculptors and Gravers, London

16th, Spring

n 123   The Cock   Mrs W. Russell

Autumn Exhibition of Modern Art, Liverpool
44th

n 636   The Spangled Cock   John A. Holms
n 688   The White Cock   J. J. Spencer
n 691   Circus   W. G. Gardiner

1915

Paisley Art Institute

39th, February–March

n 219	Huntsman and Dogs	George Burrell
n 223	Barnet Fair	George Burrell

Royal Glasgow Institute of the Fine Arts

54th

n 465	The Cock	Mrs W. W. Russell
n 469	The White Cock	J. J. Spencer

1916

Loan Exhibition of Works by Joseph Crawhall and Niels M. Lund, Laing Art Gallery, Newcastle upon Tyne

n 1	Dudie	Mrs Clay
n 2	Switzerland	John Lavery
n 3	Sketch	Mrs Clay
n 4	Sketch	F. Challoner
n 5	Cock and Hen	John Lavery
n 6	Calf	F. C. Gardiner
n 7	Ducks in a Burn(oil)	F. Challoner
n 8	Joseph Crawhall on Dan Dancer	John Lavery
n 9	Sketch	Mrs Dickinson
n 10	A Gentleman of Birmingham	Mrs Clay
n 11	Elephant	Mrs Clay
n 12	The Race	F. Challoner
n 13	Donkeys, Tangier	W. F. Henderson
n 14	The Huntsman	Richard Walton
n 15	Sketch	Mrs Dickinson
n 16	Bullfight	F. C. Gardiner
n 17	Huntsman	John J. Cowan
n 18	Camel	F. Challoner
n 19	Sketch	Mrs Clay
n 20	The Fishmonger's Pony	John J. Cowan
n 21	Goats at Tangier	F. C. Gardiner
n 22	Sketch	Mrs Clay
n 23	Fox and Geese	Richard Walton
n 24	The Cow	W. B. Paterson
n 25	Greyhounds	John J. Cowan
n 26	The White Cock	J. J. Spencer
n 27	The Farm	Mrs Dickinson
n 28	The Dogs	Richard Walton
n 29	The Butcher's Boy	W. B. Paterson
n 30	Circus	W. G. Gardiner
n 31	Sketch	Mrs Clay
n 32	The Chase	Mrs Clay
n 33	Huntsman and Hounds	John J. Cowan
n 34	Race Course	J. J. Spencer
n 35	Horses	F. Challoner
n 36	Piccadilly. Night.	John Lavery
n 37	Rapid Sketch of Arab	Mrs Wood
n 38	Rabbits	Mrs Dickinson
n 39	Japanese Goose	John J. Cowan
n 40	Sketch	Mrs Clay
n 41	Rapid Sketch of Bullfight	Mrs Wood
n 42	Study	Mrs Dickinson
n 43	The Crocodile	F. Challoner
n 44	Race Course	Mrs Clay
n 45	Donkey	F. C. Gardiner
n 46	The Farmer's Boy	John J. Cowan
n 47	Farmyard	Mrs Clay
n 48	Rabbits	Richard Walton
n 49	Circus	Mrs Clay
n 50	Dogs	Mrs Dickinson
n 51	Sketches of Horses	Mrs Dickinson
n 52	Pigs	Mrs Crawhall
n 53	Morpeth Hounds (oil)	W. F. Henderson
n 54	Pansy and Spider's Web	Mrs Wood
n 55	Dogs	Mrs Dickinson
n 56	Sketch	Mrs Clay
n 57	Fox and Pigs	Richard Walton
n 58	The Water Jump	John Lavery
n 59	Camel	Mrs Crawhall
n 60	Tiger	Richard Crawhall
n 61	The Cow	Richard Walton
n 62	Sketch	Mrs Dickinson
n 63	Sketch	F. Challoner
n 64	Frog	H. C. Fairfax-Cholmeley
n 65	Illustrations for Reynard the Fox, Reproductions	W. B. Paterson

1917

Royal Glasgow Institute of the Fine Arts

56th

n 556	The Duck Pond

1918

Paisley Art Institute

42nd, March–April

n 165	White Drake	W. A. Coats

1919

Paisley Art Institute

43rd

n 251	Pigeons	A. F. Mackean

1920

Paisley Art Institute

44th, March–April

n 245	The Magpie	W. A. Coats
n 268	Barnet Fair	George Burrell
n 276	Huntsman and Hounds	George Burrell

1922

Autumn Exhibition of Modern Art, Liverpool

50th

n 337	The Bullfinches	W. A. Coats
n 342	The Mallard	W. A. Coats
n 344	A Trout	W. A. Coats

1923

Royal Scottish Society of Painters in Watercolours,
Edinburgh

43rd

| n 210 | The Finish | John Warrack |
| n 265 | John Peel | John Warrack |

1924

Loan Exhibition of the Burrell Collection
National Gallery, Millbank, London

Fourteen works listed – see Appendix 5

Paisley Art Institute

48th, January–March

| n 381 | The Hansom Cab | John Keppie |
| n 383 | The Biter Bitten | Alexander Reid |

1925

New English Art Club, Retrospective Exhibition and 71st

January–February

| n 239 | The Spangled Cock | D. W. Cargill |

Inaugural Loan Exhibition, Kirkcaldy Museum and Art
Gallery

June–September

n 125	The Finish	John Warrack
n 134	Pigsticking n.2	John Nairn
n 135	Gibraltar Cabby	William Burrell
n 136	Elephant and Circus Pony	William Burrell
n 137	Piebald, Driving	John Nairn
n 139	Racehorses and Jockeys	William Burrell
n 140	Fishes in Aquarium (pastel)	William Burrell

1927

W. A. Coats Collection of Pictures, Galleries of Royal
Society of British Artists, London

January

Forty-six works listed – see Appendix 4

Autumn Exhibition of Modern Art, Liverpool

55th

| n 501 | The Duck Pond | J. Whitelaw Hamilton |
| n 534 | Barnet Fair | Dr Arnold E. Jones |

Royal Scottish Society of Painters in Watercolours,
Edinburgh

47th

| n 288 | Pride | Miss Robb |

1928

Second Inaugural Loan Exhibition, Scottish and Foreign
Artists, Museum and Art Gallery, Kirkcaldy

| n 1 | Goats | Sir F. C. Gardiner |
| n 2 | Pigsticking No. 2 | Miss Nairn |

n 3	Chinese Goose	Sir William Burrell
n 4	Pigsticking No. 1	Miss Nairn
n 5	Old Horse	W. G. Gardiner
n 6	A Donkey	Sir F. C. Gardiner
n 7	Sketch Drawing of a Horse	Mrs Guthrie Gardiner
n 8	The American Jockey	Sir William Burrell
n 9	The Piebald Driving	Miss Nairn
n 10	Circus Girl	Sir William Burrell
n 11	The Spangled Cock	D. W. T. Cargill
n 12	Huntsman and Hounds	Leonard Gow
n 13	A Sangar in Morocco	Jas. A. Morrice
n 14	The Farmer's Boy	Sir William Burrell
n 15	Bull Fight, San Roque	Sir William Burrell
n 16	The Black Rabbit	Mrs George Burrell
n 17	Elephant and Pony	Sir William Burrell
n 18	The Whip	National Gallery of Scotland
n 19	Dogs on Leash	Sir William Burrell
n 20	Pigsticking	J. S. M. Ressich
n 21	The Canter	Mr and Mrs James L. Caw
n 22	Four-in-Hand	William McInnes
n 23	The Duckpond	J. Whitelaw Hamilton
n 24	Circus	W. G. Gardiner
n 25	The Huntsman	Glasgow Gallery
n 26	Old Dick	James A. Morrice
n 27	Pigeons in a Cage	W. G. Gardiner
n 28	The Bull Fight	Sir F. C. Gardiner
n 29	Carriage Horses	J. P. Kinghorn
n 30	Huntsman	Mrs Guthrie Gardiner
n 31	The Camel	Mr and Mrs James L. Caw

Paisley Art Institute

52nd

| n 366 | The Tiger | T. H. Coats |

1929

Watercolours and Drawings by Contemporary Artists,
W. B. Paterson Gallery, London

| n 13 | Huntsman and Hounds | |

North East Coast Exhibition, Palace of Arts, Newcastle

May–October

n 168	Five sketches	Mrs J. Clay
n 184	Felton Races	Armstrong College
n 188	Drawing	Armstrong College
n 191	Drawing	Wm. Henderson
n 192	Drawing	Armstrong College
n 194	Drawing	Armstrong College
n 438	Donkey Boy at Algiers	W. F. Henderson
n 445	The Meet	Glasgow Art Galleries
n 446	Foxhounds, Jingling Gate	Glasgow Art Galleries

Original Drawings, W. B. Paterson Gallery, London

October

n 6	The Challenge
n 8	The Old Hunter
n 12	After the Stroke
n 19	Summer. Red Deer in Doñana.
n 21	Autumn. Roaring.
n 26	Red Deer in the Coto Doñana, Spain
n 27	The Spanish Bull Fight
n 30	Fox Hounds
n 33	Wild Boar
n 35	Ewes and Lambs
n 38	Spanish Bull Fight
n 39	Ape and Hare
n 40	Spring. Red Deer in Doñana.

1930

Royal Glasgow Institute of the Fine Arts

69th

| n 583 | The Spangled Cock |

Autumn Exhibition of Modern Art, Liverpool

58th

| n 663 | Calf | Mrs Richard Walton |

1931

Paisley Art Institute

55th, January–March

| n 255 | The Spangled Cock | D. W. T. Cargill |

Royal Glasgow Institute of the Fine Arts

70th

| n 621 | Kempton Park |

Drawings and Watercolours by British Artists
W. B. Paterson Gallery, London

December–January 1932

n 5	Ape and Hare
n 12	Foxhounds
n 30	Spanish Bull Fight
n 34	Bull Fight, After the Stroke
n 40	Summer, Red Deer in Doñana, Spain
n 44	Autumn Roaring, Red Deer in Doñana, Spain

1932

Paisley Art Institute

56th, February–March

| n 221 | A Mallard | Major John A. Coats |
| n 277 | White Drake | Thomas Heywood Coats |

1934

Paisley Art Institute

58th, January–March

| n 263 | Moorhen | Thomas Heywood Coats |

1935

Paisley Art Institute

59th, January–March

| n 222 | The French Cab Horse | Thomas Heywood Coats |
| n 228 | The Four in Hand | Thomas Heywood Coats |

A Century of Art in Glasgow, 1835–1935, Glasgow Art Gallery

May–June

n 62	Collie (oil)	Dr J. F. Barr
n 63	A Hansom Cab	Sir Thomas Dunlop
n 64	Donkeys (oil)	D. W. T. Cargill
n 66	Wag (oil)	D. W. T. Cargill
n 67	A Goat (pastel)	Sir William Burrell
n 69	Sporting Subject	Thomas H. Coats
n 70	Cock and Hen	Sir John Lavery
n 71	A White Drake	Thomas H. Coats
n 72	Foxhounds	D. W. T. Cargill
n 73	A Donkey	D. W. T. Cargill
n 75	A Chinese Goose	Sir William Burrell
n 76	Spangled Cock	D. W. T. Cargill
n 77	A Moorhen	Thomas A. Coats
n 79	Owl and Bees	Corporation of Glasgow
n 80	Starting the Buck	Thomas H. Coats
n 81	A Tiger	Thomas H. Coats
n 82	Portrait of Mary Auras	Thomas H. Coats
n 83	Polo Ball on Toast	Corporation of Glasgow
n 84	The Meet	Corporation of Glasgow
n 85	A Bull Fight	Sir Frederick C. Gardiner
n 86	Racehorse and Jockey	D. W. T. Cargill
n 87	A Minorca Cock	Sir William Burrell
n 88	The Racecourse	D. W. T. Cargill
n 89	A Moorish Packhorse, Tangier	Corporation of Glasgow
n 90	A Mallard Rising from the Water	Thomas H. Coats
n 91	Ape and Hare	D. W. T. Cargill
n 92	Goats, Tangier	Sir Frederick C. Gardiner
n 93	A Cock Pheasant	Thomas H. Coats
n 94	The Four-in-Hand	Thomas H. Coats
n 95	The Huntsman	Corporation of Glasgow
n 97–106	The Dodo and other Nursery Studies for Eileen	Lady Sempill
n 107	A Lady Alighting from a Hansom Cab	Thomas H. Coats
n 108	A French cab-horse	Thomas H. Coats
n 111	Dogs	D. W. T. Cargill
n 112	Rabbits	D. W. T. Cargill
n 113	Fox and Pigs	D. W. T. Cargill
n 114	A Cow	D. W. T. Cargill
n 119	Foxhounds – Jingling Gate	Corporation of Glasgow

1938

Empire Exhibition, Palace of Arts, Glasgow

May–October

n 191	Hounds	D. W. T. Cargill
n 193	The Dove	Tate, London
n 194	Flower Shop	A. T. Reid
n 195	Spangled Cock	D. W. T. Cargill
n 196	White Drake	T. H. Coats
n 197	Four in Hand: Flea Bitten Grey	W. McInnes
n 198	Mallard Rising off Water	T. H. Coats
n 199	Kempton Park	L. Harper Gow
n 200	An Arab Raid	A. T. Reid
n 203	Huntsman	A. C. J. Wall
n 205	Owl	A. C. J. Wall
n 207	Huntsman and Hounds	A. C. J. Wall
n 210	Mare and Foal	A. C. J. Wall
n ?	White Cow	A. C. J. Wall

1939

Exhibition of Scottish Art, Royal Academy, London

January–March

n 652	Mallard Rising from Water	T. H. Coats
n 653	Hounds	D. W. T. Cargill
n 654	Casting Hounds	L. Harper Gow
n 655	Spangled Cock	D. W. T. Cargill
n 656	White Drake	T. H. Coats
n 657	Flower Shop	A. T. Reid
n 658	Four in Hand	W. McInnes
n 659	Aviary	W. Burrell
n 661	Performing Dogs	W. Burrell
n 662	An Arab Ploughing	National Gallery of Scotland
n 663	The Greyhound	W. Burrell
n 664	Black Cock	W. Burrell
n 665	A Goat	National Gallery of Scotland
n 666	Bull Fight	Lady Gardiner

1940

British Painting since Whistler, National Gallery, London

March

n 259	The Cock and the Hen	Sir John Lavery
n 290	Mallard Rising from the Water	T. H. Coats
n 328	The Pig	Professor Allan Mainds
n 330	Horse by a Fence	Professor Allan Mainds
n 331	Study of two Horses	Professor Allan Mainds
n 332	Piccadilly Circus, 1888	Sir John Lavery
n 333	Felton – August	Professor Allan Mainds
n 334	Felton Races	Professor Allan Mainds
n 337	Trotting Horse	Professor Allan Mainds
n 350	Hound	A. C. J. Wall

APPENDIX 2: 1894 AND 1912 EXHIBITION CATALOGUES

A. *Catalogue of the Collected Works of Joseph Crawhall Jr.*
La Société des Beaux-Arts, 124 St Vincent Street, Glasgow, April 1894

1. In the Aviary – Clifton
2. Performing Dogs
3. The Goatherd
4. Greyhound
5. 'Plaza de Toros'
6. Barb Horse in Stable
7. Camels
8. Fiacre – Gibraltar
9. A Check
10. 'Flossie'
11. The Promenade
12. The Snake-Charmer
13. Moorish Soldier
14. Cappa
15. (No Title)
16. Picador
17. Hounds in Kennel
18. The Badger
19. Cock – Fighting
20. Spanish Bull-Ring
21. Pigeons
22. Draught Bullock
23. Barnet Fair
24. The Finish
25. Four-in-Hand
26. Bolted
27. Exercising
28. Cowboy
29. Kempton Park
30. Huntsman – Tangier
31. Overmantel
32. The Smithy
33. Goats at Tangier
34. Donkey
35. Bull-Ring – Algeciras
36. Circus
37. (No Title)
38. Huntsman
39. Huntsman with Hounds
40. Fishing
41. Wild Duck
42. The Inn Door
43. Fox-Hunting
44. (No Title)
45. Cub-Hunting
46. Bull-Ring
47. The Goat
48. Cat and Canary
49. Riot
50. Canary
51. A Wattle Fence
52. Picador
53. Caricature
54. Ware Hare
55. Hansom-Cab
56. Donkeys – Spain
57. Pack Mules
58. Master of Harriers
59. Polo-Pony
60. Sunlight
61. Cat and Flowerpot
62. Morning Promenade
63. Hen and Chickens (pastel)
64. Spanish Muleteer
65. Farm Labourer with Horse
66. Rat with Egg
67. Hussar
68. 'Un Chasseur Français'
69. Picadors
70. 'The Hare and the Tortoise'
71. A Spring Meeting
72. 'Kitty'
73. The Finish
74. A Spill
75. Horse Drinking
76. White Cock
77. Horse in Shed
78. The 'Row'
79. Hound Sleeping
80. Bull-Ring

Lenders:

Miss Croall
T. G. Arthur
George Burrell
William Burrell
James Cox Cox
James Gardiner
James Garroway
John Keppie
A. J. Kirkpatrick
Laurence Pullar
J. J. Spencer

B. *Catalogue of a Loan Collection of Water Colour Drawings by Joseph Crawhall*
Wm. B. Paterson, 5 Old Bond Street, London, May and June 1912

1. Doves
2. The Jackdaw (illustr.)
3. The Picador
4. The Rook's Nest
5. A Spanish Water Carrier
6. The Farmer's Boy
7. The Pony Fair
8. The Mallard
9. Ewes and Lambs
10. The Magpie
11. The Coach (illustr.)
12. Pigeons
13. The White Drake
14. The Black Rabbit (illustr.)
15. Picador No. 2 (illustr.)
16. The Chinese Goose
17. Racehorses
18. The Horse Pond
19. A Bull Fight
20. The Circus Rider
21. The Black Cock (illustr.)
22. Two Rabbits
23. The Aviary, Clifton
24. Performing Dogs
25. The Spangled Cock
26. Pigeon
27. Barnet Fair
28. American Jockeys (illustr.)
29. The Cow
30. A Paris Cab
31. The Pheasant
32. Mare and Foal
33. The Hansom Cab
34. Chantecler and the Funerayles of Coppen
35. A Red Indian
36. Corbant the Roke and Reynarde
37. The Huntsman
38. Rukenawe the she Ape counsels the Foxe
39. The Dog Cart
40. Ysegrym the Wulf and the Mare
41. The Goat
42. Huntsman and Hounds
43. Courtoys the Hounde
44. The Slipper
45. The Bear and the Honey
46. The Whipper In
47. Bellyn the Ramme, Kywart the Hare, and Reynarde the Foxe
48. The Polo Pony
49. Tybert the Catte in the Gryn
50. The Row

APPENDIX 3: ALEXANDER REID–JOSEPH CRAWHALL CORRESPONDENCE

With the exception of one or two letters in the possession of the Crawhall family and a handful of letters found pasted or placed into his father's commonplace books few letters written by Joseph Crawhall are known to have survived. Fortunately twenty-three letters, dating from the period 1900–4, written to Crawhall's dealer, Alexander Reid, have been preserved. These valuable documents form part of the archive of the late Dr T. J. Honeyman deposited in the Manuscript Department of the National Library of Scotland, Edinburgh. The text of these letters is given as the letters provide valuable information on Crawhall's attitude to notions of finish, framing and exhibiting. They also demonstrate that, contrary to much that has been written by earlier writers, Crawhall was concerned that he was paid fairly for his work.

Aug 190[0]   Beacon Banks, Nr Easingwold, Yorks
Dear Alec,
Just a line to say that I sent off the 5 black and white pig-sticking drawings about a week ago and should like to know if you have got them   yrs ever   J Crawhall.

Nov 1900   Beacon Banks, Nr Easingwold, Yorks
Dear Alec,
Many thanks for cheque, altho I certainly think the price an absurd one, however as you say you have a number, and I conclude don't want any more I must dispose of them elsewhere. I find I have been throwing my work away and I must say I don't think you have treated me quite fairly as the prices I have received compared with the prices you get, are out of all character, however as you have raised the question it leaves me free to do the best for myself   yrs sincerely J Crawhall

Nov 24 1900   Beacon Banks, Nr Easingwold, Yorks
Dear Alec,
to plunge at once in 'media res' you say that 'I have made the prices myself', remember you have repeatedly written to say that you can't give so much, the matter of slight drawings is rather difficult because I have so often found that I have accepted a low price for a drawing you considered slight, and afterwards been asthonished [sic] to find that it has brought a better price than a finished one.

However as you say you must have a profit on something which seems reasonable, and I have no wish to sell my work elsewhere provided, I get a fair price, I go to Teddy's tomorrow.   Love to all,   yrs ever,   J Crawhall.

[1901]   Beacon Banks, Nr Easingwold, Yorks
Dear Alec,
I returned the paper to the [illegible] of the International Glasgow mentioning
1. The Black Cock   2. Black Rabbit
3. Pigeon
I think that will do if we can get them, I did not know Burrell's address but I have no doubt they will know it.

You asked about the price of the black and white I thought about £60. In any case you might send me £50 to be going on with, as I am going away for a bit, to stay with Teddy. I hope to be able to send you a [illegible] soon, I have two that have been on the stocks for some time but contrary to my usual custom I have not burnt them. You did not mention anything about the doings of the talent in Glasgow so I assume nothing of vital importance is going on. Is old Tom still alive? How are the horses, have you the same or new ones? When you write you can tell me any news.

Winter is about to commence here we had snow the other day. I do hope we will not have a repetition of last year. Love to all   yrs ever   J Crawhall.

May 3 1901   Beacon Banks, Nr Easingwold, Yorks
Dear Alec,
I want you to send me two frames, white of a good design and I will send them back full. Sizes 15 × 12½ and 18 and 11½. I have the drawings nearly complete ie., out of danger and not the worst I have done either. I did some low reliefs of animals and coloured them, but more for amusement than anything else, some day you may see them. I hope to be in Glasgow to see the show before it closes and hope to have the pleasure of seeing you in the meantime with best regards to yours,   yrs   J Crawhall.

May 10 1901   Beacon Banks, Nr Easingwold, Yorks
Dear Alec,
I want you to send me £30 as I find I have to go to London on the 16th. please let me have it before that date. I will send off the two drawings as soon as the frames arrive, they are both well finished, and I should like to exhibit them in London in the autumn International if you can make an arrangement to that effect.   yrs in haste   J Crawhall.

[1901]   Beacon Banks, Nr Easingwold, Yorks
Dear Alec,
I want to know if you can get me two pictures to exhibit at the International. I should like the White Duck and the horses on the hill that Arthur has you know the two [sketch of White Drake and sketch of Horse Fair]. I shall also send

what I have here. You might let me know as soon as possible as the bally things have to be by the 12 Sep. One of these I have here is a ripper the other not so interesting but safe. yrs in great haste.   J Crawhall

[1901]   Beacon Banks, Nr Easingwold, Yorks
Dear Alec,
I am sorry the 'duck' owner is such a badger certainly don't run any risk of insult again. If you can get Arthur's it will do quite well, Burrell's horse fair was shown last time. I may mention that I had nò intention of sending the drawings here 'for sale' as I think I promised you the refusal of all work some time since, as you said if you were prepared to give as much as anyone else you were entitled to the chance, to which I quite agreed.

I am quite of your opinion that showing is not of any great use to me, but this is exceptional as I think the show mostly of support. I promised to contribute when possible. Let me know as soon as you can   yrs ever   J Crawhall

Aug 10 [1901]   Beacon Banks, Nr Easingwold, Yorks
Dear Alec,
I have been anxiously waiting to hear from you as to whether you were successful in getting the drawing from Arthur or not. I hope so as the time is getting short. I go to London on the 13 to help in hanging you might let me know as soon as possible (wire if necessary). I am taking a drawing from here finished all right and good. Failing Arthur what else is there to be had of some size? How about Garroway's pastel, here you know, it is a fair size and tho old is not bad. Please let me know as soon as you can   yrs in haste   J Crawhall

Dec 2, 1901   Beacon Banks, Nr Easingwold, Yorks
Dear Alec,
Just a line to ask if you want the drawing of the Jackdaw in International as the show closes next week   yrs ever   in haste   J Crawhall

[1901]   Beacon Banks, Nr Easingwold, Yorks.
Dear Alec,
tho late accept compliments
   I presume C.C. stands for County Council or Cricket Club. The price of the Jackdaw is £65 sixty five, I have some drawings at present being reproduced in colour and when I get them back you can have them if you like   yrs in haste J Crawhall.

[1902]   Beacon Banks, Nr Easingwold, Yorks
Dear Alec,
Many thanks for cheque. I will let you have the drawings as soon as the printers have done with them, I wrote about them but have not yet had an answer, they are much cheaper than the John Dow, one is very good. I will square up the bill either by a reduction or drawing or by sketch have nothing completed here at present but am likely to have soon I am afraid I can't get North at present altho [illegible] with your hounds is [illegible] hunting is off here very hard frost.   yrs ever   J Crawhall.

[1902]   Beacon Banks, Nr Easingwold, Yorks
Dear Alec,
With regard to the price of the two drawings you can just send me what you think fair, after deducting the bill, I am much interested in my big one, in great haste,   yrs ever, J Crawhall.

[1902]   Beacon Banks, Nr Easingwold, Yorks
Dear Alec,
I thought you would be wondering why the drawings had not arrived, but the alterations in the size meant rather more than I expected but there is no fear of them, and I will send them as soon as possible.   Best regards,   in great haste, yrs   J Crawhall

August 29, 1902, York
Sent the pony off at the same time hope it is all right.

[1902]   Beacon Banks, Nr Easingwold, Yorks
Dear Alec,
The drawings are as you thought for publication in a Magazine and not for sale. The Connoisseur man wanted some, one is pretty good for a novice. You can send along the balance after deducting £30 I owe you, if convenient, and even if not. I am pleased to know you are at least as respectable as Teddy used to be, but you always were   yrs in haste   J Crawhall

[1903]   Beacon Banks, Nr Easingwold, Yorks
Dear Alec,
I was quite under the impression that I had sent you the price of the two drawings what do you say to £100, I think the cock is fairly good. By all means cut the big drawing down as you suggest, only burn the remainder. I will send you a small one to make up for the difference. If you agree to the price you might send me on some of it as I am somewhat low in funds.   Yours ever,   J Crawhall.

[1903]   Beacon Banks
Dear Alec,
I did not understand that the pony was to be thrown in with the other two, however if that was the arrangement I suppose it must stand. I hope you have put the 'Cock' into a wide white mount, I tried it with one and it looked well it is a drawing I am rather fond of, and mind don't sell it to anyone who objects to let you have it to exhibit if you think of having a show next year. You remember that chap WOOD you met here, he has had a very bad fall and got smashed up. You can send me £50 of the £80 as soon as convenient as I am in need of some ready.

[1903]   Brandsby, Nr Easingwold, Yorks
Dear Alec,
Many thanks. I will be at the Whistler dinner am taking a friend, but hope to see you there   yrs ever   J Crawhall

[1903]   Brandsby, Nr Easingwold, Yorks

Dear Alec,

Many thanks, received all right. I don't think the drawings ever appeared at least not that I am aware of, and I must try to get the third one back. I will see what I can do with the [illegible] but at present it is not with us, moving having upset things a bit. I expect Hornel's show will be very interesting, glad to hear business is looking up, you never said how the silver Spangled Cock looked in a frame.   yrs ever,   J Crawhall.

[1903]   Brandsby, Easingwold, Yorks

Dear Alec,

When you have time you might let me know if you can secure a decent exhibit of my work for the International in Dec you said you could get the Reynard drawings from Arthur, and that last spotted cock I think would do, I hope to have some new work ready, but can't count upon that, as I would not hurry myself for exhibition.   Regards to all,   yrs ever, J Crawhall.

[1903]   Brandsby, Easingwold, Yorks

Dear Alec,

I think you said you could get the Silver Spangled Hamburgh, black and white cock in other words for the International show, do you know about the sending in day, I have another picture here a very good one not quite finished. I think the two will do all right. I saw Teddy the other day and he told me you were leaving your place, I did not quite understand whether you were giving up business altogether, or just making a change. You might let me know if the drawing will be sent, this one [sketch of Spangled Cock], you know,   yrs ever,   J Crawhall.

[1904]   Brandsby, Nr. Easingwold, Yorks

Dear Alec,

Just a line to ask if you can send me on the £25 left over, I think you said that was the amount. We have not got into our new house yet, but hope to soon. It seems a long time since I have heard of or from you write with your news at your leisure,   yrs ever,   J Crawhall.

APPENDIX 4: W.A.COATS COLLECTION

(The provenance of works by Joseph Crawhall formerly in the collection of W. A. Coats up to and including 1935)

The numbers and titles are from the *Catalogue of Pictures and Drawings Being the Entire Collection of the late W. A. Coats, Esqre*. Exhibited at the Galleries of the Royal Society of British Artists, Suffolk Street, London. Exhibition organised by Wm. B. Paterson, 5 Old Bond Street, London. January 1927.

The copy in italics indicates only those works sold through the dealer Wm. B. Paterson during or after the 1927 exhibition; and at Christie's on 12 April, 1935. Lot number, sale price and purchaser (dealer) are noted for each work included in the Christie's sale.

1. Bullfinches. *Christie's lot n. 23. 135 guineas to J. B. Bennett & Sons*
2. Mary Auras.
3. Tybert the Catte in the Gryn. *Christie's lot n. 8 (part lot). 320 guineas to A. Reid & Lefevre*
4. A Terrier. *Wm. B. Paterson*
5. A Moor Hen.
6. Cab Horse. *Christie's lot n. 20. 58 guineas to J. B. Bennett & Sons*
7. Chantecler and the Funerales of Coppen. *Christie's lot n. 8 (part lot). 320 guineas to A. Reid & Lefevre*
8. Trout Rising. *Christie's lot n. 19. 160 guineas to I. McNicol*
9. The White Drake.
10. Starting the Buck.
11. Courtoys the Hounde. *Christie's lot n. 8 (part lot). 320 guineas to A. Reid & Lefevre*
12. The Hunt. *Wm. B. Paterson*
13. Four in Hand.
14. Mary in Spain. *Wm. B. Paterson*
15. Ysegryn the Wulf and the Mare. *Christie's lot n. 8 (part lot). 320 guineas to A. Reid & Lefevre*
16. The Showman.
17. A Pheasant. *Christie's lot n. 10. 380 guineas*
18. The Horse Pond. *Christie's lot n. 14. 45 guineas to I. McNicol*
19. Belyn the Ramme, Kywart the Hare, and Reynarde the Foxe. *Christie's lot n. 8 (part lot). 320 guineas to A. Reid & Lefevre*
20. The Tiger.
21. The Circus. *Wm. B. Paterson*
22. The Magpie. *Wm. B. Paterson*
23. Rukenaw the She Ape Counsels the Foxe. *Christie's lot n. 8 (part lot). 320 guineas to A. Reid & Lefevre*
24. Mare and Foal. *Christie's lot n. 18. 50 guineas to I. McNicol*
25. The Jockeys. *Christie's lot n. 9. 38 guineas to I. McNicol*
26. The Rabbits. *Christie's lot n. 22. 50 guineas to J. B. Bennett & Sons*
27. How Bruyn the Bear Ate the Honey. *Christie's lot n. 8 (part lot). 320 guineas to A. Reid & Lefevre*
28. Donkeys, Tangier. *Christie's lot n. 24. 70 guineas to A. Reid & Lefevre*
29. The Hansom Cab. *Christie's lot n. 11. 110 guineas to J. B. Bennett & Sons*
30. Lady on Horseback. *Wm. B. Paterson*
31. Sheep in Pasture. *Wm. B. Paterson*
32. The Foxe and the Wulf's Wife. *Christie's lot n. 8 (part lot). 320 guineas to A. Reid & Lefevre*
33. Pig Sticking. *Christie's lot n. 16. 95 guineas to A. Reid & Lefevre*
34. Race Horses and Jockeys. *Christie's lot n. 15. 100 guineas to I. McNicol*
35. Paris Cab.
36. The Foxe and the Capone. *Christie's lot n. 8 (part lot). 320 guineas to A. Reid & Lefevre*
37. The Polo Player. *Christie's lot n. 17. 45 guineas*
38. The Rabbit Warren. *Wm. B. Paterson*
39. The Mallard. *Christie's lot n. 7. 1,150 guineas to J. B. Bennett & Sons*
40. Corbart the Roke and Reynarde. *Christie's lot n. 8 (part lot). 320 guineas to A. Reid & Lefevre*
41. The Goat. *Wm. B. Paterson*
42. Mary in Switzerland. *Wm. B. Paterson*
43. Water Carrier. *Christie's lot n. 21. 32 guineas to Aitken Dott*
44. The Bull Fight. *Christie's lot n. 12. 400 guineas*
45. The Sportsman's Dream.
46. Picador II. *Christie's lot no. 13. 60 guineas*

APPENDIX 5: SIR WILLIAM BURRELL'S CRAWHALL PURCHASES, 1916-52

A. Loan Exhibition of the Burrell Collection, National Gallery, Millbank, 1924

This exhibition included eighteen works by Joseph Crawhall:

n 90	Barnet Fair	n 96	The Old Cow	n 117	The American Jockey
n 91	The Chinese Goose	n 112	Bull Fight	n 118	Greyhound
n 92	The Farmer's Boy	n 113	The Goat	n 124	The Goatherd
n 93	The Aviary	n 114	The Pigeon	n 125	Camels
n 94	The Minorca Cock	n 115	The Black Cock	n 127	The Whipper-In
n 95	Picketed Horses, Tangier, 1888	n 116	The Rook's Nest	n 132	Indian on Horseback

B. Summary of Crawhall Acquisitions as Recorded in Sir William Burrell's Purchase Books

1916: 1 : The American Jockey
1917: 2 : The Old Cow
The Rook's Nest (half interest purchased from George Burrell)
1918: 4 : Untitled
The Meet
The Chinese Goose
The Farmer's Boy
1919: 1 : Saddle Horses
1920: 1 : The Winner
1921: 6 : Minorca Cock
Jingling Gate
Galloway Goat
Three untitled pen and ink drawings
1922:51 : Paris, Hansom Cab
Dogs
The Whipper-In
Indian on Horseback
The Road Hog
Crawhall Rearing on Horseback
Piper and Cats
Mary Napoleon
Ducks and Worm
Forty-two untitled drawings
1923: 2 : Horses Resting
Mules

1924: 5 : Owl and Bees
Elephant and Circus Pony
Study of Horses
Horses in Stable
Girl Cycling
1926: 5 : The Bullring, San Roque
Ayr Races – The Newmarket Prophet
Huntsman and Hounds
Fishmonger's Pony
Greyhounds on Leash
1927: 6 : The Circus
Arab Horseman on Beach with Dog
The Earth Stopper
Kempton Park
French Cavalry Officer
Lady on Horseback
1928: 2 : The Circus Rider
The Magpie
1930: 1 : The Meet
1932: 1 : Two Pigeons on a Roof
1933: 1 : The Governess Cart
1935: 11: Set of ten illustrations: Reynard the Fox
The Rabbits
1936: 1 : The Spanish Cock with Snail

1938: 6 : Study of birds and animals
A Rabbit
Farmer on Horseback
Mules on Sand at Tangier
Black Spanish Cock
A Calf
1942: 4 : The Flower Shop
An Arab Raid
Donkeys on Sand at Tangier
A Preliminary Canter
1944: 2 : Mother Duck and Three Ducklings
Two Soldiers in Red Tunic
1945: 2 : The Race
Tigers
1947: 1 : Donkeys Tethered to a Tree
1948: 5 : Reproduction of Spangled Cock
Tiger Feasting
Girl feeding Poultry
Municipal Guards
Camel
1951: 1 : Two Jockeys on Horseback
1952: 1 : Goats on Hillside, Tangier

INDEX

The pages on which illustrations appear are given in *italics*.